A QUAKER BOOK
OF WISDOM

A QUAKER BOOK OF WISDOM

LIFE LESSONS IN
SIMPLICITY, SERVICE, AND COMMON SENSE

ROBERT LAWRENCE SMITH

EAGLE BROOK
WILLIAM MORROW AND COMPANY, INC.
NEW YORK

A LIVING PLANET BOOK

Published by Eagle Brook
An Imprint of William Morrow and Company, Inc.
1350 Avenue of the Americas, New York, N.Y. 10019

QUILT PHOTO CREDITS: All photographs courtesy of Brandywine River Museum. **Prologue**: Album friendship bedquilt, 1848–49. Made by Rachel Spencer Michener and James Michener, Chester County, PA. Collection of Donald and Barbara Pusey. **Ch. 1**: Courthouse steps pattern bedquilt, 1868. Made by Martha Potts Mather for Martha Potts Mitchell, Bucks County, PA. Collection of Elizabeth R. W. Lukshides, descendant of the Mather-Parry family. **Ch. 2**: Reel pattern (variant) friendship bedquilt, circa 1840–45. Made by or for Susanna Cox, Chester County, PA. Collection of Nancy F. Donaldson, great-granddaughter of Susanna Cox. **Ch. 3**: Ohio Star, or Ribbon Star, pattern friendship bedquilt, circa 1846. Made by or for Ann Gibson Dixon. Kingsessing, PA. Owned by her great-great-granddaughter Margaret Rhein Williams. **Ch. 4**: Two-Patch Triangles, or Thousands of Triangles, pattern doll's quilt, circa 1840–60. Attributed to Sarah E. Roberts Evans or her daughter Lydia, Burlington County, NJ. Collection of Mrs. S. Kendrick Eshleman III. **Ch. 5**: Star of Lemoyne pattern bedquilt, 1843. Attributed to Ann Wickersham, Chester County, PA. Collection of Anna Walton Myers. **Ch. 6**: Album friendship bedquilt, circa 1845–48. Attributed to Abigail Maule, Chester County, PA, Private Collection. **Ch. 7**: Four-Patch Sash and Block pattern bedquilt, circa 1840–60, Sarah W. Sharp, Burlington County, NJ. Collection of Mrs. S. Kendrick Eshleman III. **Ch. 8**: Star of Bethlehem, or Lone Star, pattern bedquilt, circa 1844, Sarah Pusey, Chester County, PA. Collection of Nancy and Gary Plumley. **Ch. 9**: Four-Patch pattern doll's quilt, circa 1860–80. Attributed to a member of the Mather-Parry family, Bucks County, PA. Collection of Elizabeth R. W. Lukshides, descendant of the Mather-Parry family. **Ch. 10**: Star of Bethlehem, or Lone Star, pattern bedquilt, circa 1840–60. Descended in the Jarrett family, Montgomery Country, PA. Quilt belongs to the Jarrett family, Montgomery Country, PA. **Epilogue**: Courtesy of the Mercer Museum of The Bucks County Historical Society.

Library of Congress Cataloging-in-Publication Data

Smith, Robert Lawrence, 1924–
    A Quaker book of wisdom : life lessons in simplicity, service, and common sense / by Robert Lawrence Smith.—1st ed.
        p.   cm.
    ISBN 0-688-15653-3 (alk. paper)
    1. Christian life—Quaker authors.   2. Spiritual life—Society of Friends.   I. Title.
BX7738.S55   1998
248.4'896—dc21
                                                                98-16294
                                                                CIP

Printed in the United States of America

First Edition

1   2   3   4   5   6   7   8   9   10

BOOK DESIGN BY M. E. CHALLINOR

www.williammorrow.com

For my wife, Eliza,
and for my children, Susie, Katie & Geoff

CONTENTS

PROLOGUE

LET YOUR LIFE SPEAK

WHEN I WAS THIRTEEN my maternal grandfather wrote a monograph tracing three centuries of his Quaker family's life in America. He titled it "Notes on My Stokes Ancestry," and in his preface he explained the reasons for his undertaking. "With the passing of each generation," Grandfather Stokes wrote, "much that has come down by way of tradition in the history of a family is irretrievably lost, so it seems well to gather up such facts as are stored in memory or obtained in research and put them into more permanent form, in the hope that they may prove interesting to my descendants."

There were no Nobel laureates in my mother's family. Although generation after generation of the Stokes family produced doctors, there were no secretaries of state, five-star generals, literary luminaries, glamorous movie stars, bank robbers, long-distance swimmers, or counterespionage agents. No one the media would consider newsworthy. Grandfather, who represented the fourth generation of Quaker physicians practicing in our small town of Moorestown, New Jersey, addressed this fact head-on. "The roll call of ancestors," he wrote, "includes no figures of outstanding importance in history." Rather, he said, what his book did provide was "a record of men and women who lived active, useful lives, and who gave to their nation and their communities the best that was in them."

By recording the well-spent lives of these virtuous folk, Grandfather Stokes hoped to provide "an example to follow, and a stimulus to do our part in the world and leave to our descendants a similar record of work well done." In encouraging new generations of the family to honor and emulate their admirable forebears, he was echoing a central message of Quakerism resoundingly set forth by George Fox, the religion's seventeenth-century founder: "Let your life speak."

I was only one of the immediate descendants that Grandfather was addressing. In addition to my mother, he and Grandmother had two sons, both of whom became doctors like their father, married, and had children of their own. These cousins and my two sisters and I brought the roster of grandchildren to eleven. Yet I read Grandfather's account as avidly as if it had been written for me alone. And I found it both instructive and inspiring. Now, a grandfather myself, I have a deeper understanding of his motives. One of the fruits of aging is the realization that our greatest possession is what we know about life. We can do no better than to pass along our most precious possessions to those most precious to us.

And that is what this little book is intended to do. It reflects at every turn the influences on my life of Quaker thought and practice—the possessions of mind and heart picked up as the son, grandson, great-grandson, brother, nephew, cousin, uncle, and father of Quakers. In writing this book, I have drawn on my own life experience as well as on the wisdom and inner journeys of a number of others—especially family members, past and present, who have vitally influenced my Quaker outlook on life. I am in some ways continuing Grandfather Stokes's message to his descendants, but I am also writing in the belief that every thinking, feeling person is reserving space inside for the sort of lasting sustenance that Quaker wisdom provides.

It is my ever-growing conviction that the compassionate Quaker message badly needs to be heard in today's complex, materialistic, often unjust, and discriminatory society. Every day brings new public debate over issues Quakers have always addressed: war and peace, social justice, education, health care, poverty, business ethics, public service, the use of world resources. The list goes on.

On a more spiritual plane, the circumstances of modern life give far too little nourishment to our common humanity—to goodness, courage, common sense, reflection, wonder, patience, understanding—to what the Greek philosopher Plato called "our mysterious preference for the best." In our frenetic strivings to compete and "succeed"—to acquire wealth and goods in a society where people are often judged by what they own and what they wear rather than who they are— how do the Quaker concepts of simplicity and truth fit in? How can the injunction to express what is best in us win the allegiance of the self-absorbed Me Generation, the rootless Generation X, and the not yet captioned generations to come?

The novelist Saul Bellow, whose humanitarian concerns were shaped by the ethical tenets of Judaism, spoke eloquently in his Nobel Prize acceptance speech of our "immense desire for certain durable human goods—truth, for instance, freedom, wisdom." It is my hope in writing this book to offer some of those "durable human goods" to my own grandchildren as well as to other young people, Quakers and non-Quakers both, as they confront the unpredictable and unforgiving terrain that lies ahead. Looking back, I realize that the major decisions we face in adolescence and youth have enormous power to creatively shape or destructively restrict our choices in later life. For me, Quaker teaching has proven a resource never failing, a home base I could rely on for guidance in making significant decisions throughout my life—but most critically in young adulthood.

I feel a good deal of hesitancy concerning my central position in this book about Quaker wisdom. Humility is simplicity of spirit, and simplicity of spirit is at the heart of Quakerism. But I am also aware that a lifetime habit of reticence and reserve may have been a disservice to my own three children. I often wonder if I could have given Susie, Katie, and Geoff more guidance as they traveled the course from childhood to adulthood had I been less reluctant to speak out plainly about the significance of their Quaker heritage. I hope that this book will help my children and grandchildren understand the Quaker values that have proven most useful to me. In any case, I now recognize that I will never get anything of worth written if I keep tripping over the humility that seeks to inform this book.

I must point out at the start that Quakerism is a pragmatic faith that depends on inner experience, on habits of mind and feeling that come from living rather than from reading. As we Quakers say, "The letter killeth, the Spirit giveth life." A Quakerly concern—how much of life can we learn from books?—remains an open question. Yet an incalculable part of what we know—a fact young people often reject—comes from familiarity, through written accounts, with the lives of those who came before us. Grandfather Stokes understood this truth, as did the authors of the Old Testament Book of Deuteronomy, who remind us, "We all warm ourselves by fires we did not build and drink from wells we did not dig."

To me, Quaker values of simplicity and silent contemplation, truth and conscience, seem more important now than ever before. So many of us today are cynical, easily bored, fearful of solitude. We are so overstimulated by the materialistic messages that advertisers convey, the incessant inconsequential chatter of talk radio and talk television, the constant roar of rock music and political rhetoric, that it is difficult to comprehend the gratifications of a simpler life. Or to understand what simplicity, in the Quaker sense, actually means. To Quakers simplicity does not mean turning the clock back on progress or rejecting the benefits of modern science and conveniences of modern technology. Nor does it mean casting off one's possessions and embracing a life of poverty. And it certainly does not mean casting off joy.

The basic humanistic Quaker precepts of valuing racial and gender equality, promoting social justice, nonviolence—and, yes, sometimes civil disobedience— seem to me so modern, so relevant to today's society, that when I thought about writing this book I was suddenly surprised that no one had written one like it. What particularly struck me is that the Quaker ideals formulated in the seventeenth century remain contemporary in every sense, and the basic injunction to "let your life speak," to live each day in accordance with these beliefs, seems totally untarnished by the passage of time.

As I set to work, I tried to hear afresh what Quakers have been saying for more than three hundred years and to give these ideas voice and meaning through examples from a life they have deeply affected. I hope that the Quaker messages distilled in these pages may be to readers what they have been to me at every turn in my life—in Isaiah's words, "as rivers of water in a dry place and as the shadow of a great rock in a weary land."

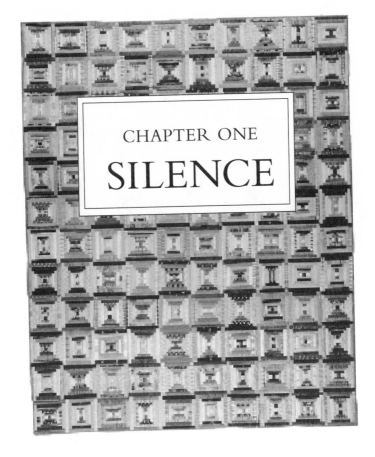

CHAPTER ONE

SILENCE

SILENCE. Even speaking the word seems to violate its meaning.

In reality, silence is almost nonexistent. If we stop speaking and turn off our telephones and televisions and radios and computers, there is always some sound of technology at work, nearby or far off. A refrigerator humming. An airplane droning overhead. A truck straining up a hill.

And if we try to escape our noisy modern world, we discover that nature is anything but silent. There is nothing so cacophonous as a meadow at dawn or a pond at sunset. The only truly silent environments are deep under water and in outer space—neither of which is particularly hospitable to human life.

Even when we sleep, we cannot escape the sound and the fury of our unconscious. Voices cry out to us from the darkness. At times our unconscious even compels us to speak in our sleep. It's as if something in nature, and in our natures, abhors the vacuum of silence and struggles mightily to fill it.

Why then, has the concept of silence been hailed as "golden" since ancient times? Why do we extol its virtues when we seem to flee from it at every turn? And what does silence mean to Quakers, who take their spiritual sustenance from a unique form of worship based on group silence?

For Quakers, wisdom begins in silence. Quakers believe that only when we have silenced our voices and our souls can we hear the "still small voice" that dwells within each of us—the voice of God that speaks to us and that we express to others through our deeds. Only by listening in stillness for that voice and letting it guide our actions can we truly let our lives speak.

Quakerism, and its unique form of silent worship, began 350 years ago with the lonely spiritual journey of an unlettered young Englishman named George Fox. Born in 1624 in the small village of Fenny Drayton in Leicestershire, he was the son of a weaver who was so esteemed for his religious fervor that he was known as a "Righteous Christer."

I can't help thinking of the young George Fox as an odd duck, a kid who didn't fit in, the last boy you'd choose for your team. From childhood on he was tormented by intense spiritual unrest. At the age of nineteen, dismayed by the shallowness of those he turned to for help, he left home and his job as a shoemaker's apprentice to wander the countryside and search for a spiritual path, for a revelation of truth he could bring into his and every other life.

It was a time of sects and schisms, an era of intense religious ferment. Dissidents from the established Protestant church were turning to offshoot religious groups that seemed to promise a more meaningful spiritual life. Among these new Christian sects were the Anabaptists, the Seekers, the Ranters, the Diggers, the Levellers. All sought in their own ways to bring religious ideas into closer harmony with the economic and spiritual lives of ordinary people. Fox conferred with their leaders, searched his own soul, and sought his own enlightenment. And after years of wandering, preaching, and imprisonment for his radical ideas about religious and social reform, his prayers were answered. As Fox wrote in his now-famous *Journal:* "When all my hopes in them [the religious leaders he'd consulted] and in all men were gone, so that I had nothing outwardly to help me, nor could I tell what to do, then, oh then, I heard a voice."

That voice was the voice of God, speaking to him directly as He had to the prophets of ancient days. The message Fox drew from his mystical experience was

4

that each individual has the capacity for direct dialogue with God, without the need for clerical intermediaries. Anyone could do it. God, he believed, appears to us through a divine inner voice, an inner light shared by all. Continuing revelation would occur if people joined together in silence and opened their hearts to the divine voice within. As Psalm 46 directs us: "Be still, and know that I am God."

George Fox's message that "there is that of God in every man" was a profoundly optimistic view of human nature. Belief in original sin was fundamental to the established Protestant church of the period, which held that all human beings were predestined to follow in the damned footsteps of Adam and Eve, irresistibly drawn to sin and temptation. Although Quakerism is firmly grounded in Christianity, Fox believed that the divine spark within all people guides them toward the good, toward the best in themselves—toward God. Therefore, all people carry within them the potential for perfectibility.

The kernel of George Fox's vision was that God finds individual expression within each of our souls and within each of our lives. It falls to us individually to seek our own inner voice and, by heeding it, "let our lives speak." For three centuries the essence of Quaker belief, Quaker faith, and Quaker action has echoed

Fox's epiphany: "There is that of God in every man."
If we can achieve stillness of spirit, God will speak to
us out of the silence.

Fox traveled widely during his lifetime and spread
his faith to ever-growing crowds of religious seekers in
England, on the Continent, and in the American colonies. Ironically, this evangelist for silent worship was
a charismatic speaker who attracted large numbers of
followers, many of them converts from other new
Christian sects. Virtually all of the other Protestant sects
that were founded in the seventeenth and eighteenth
centuries eventually died out, some very quickly and
some—like the celibate Shakers—by slow attrition. But
Quakerism thrived. Fox's followers began calling themselves "Children of Light," "Publishers of Truth,"
"Friends of Truth," and, finally, "The Religious Society of Friends," the name that is still used. They
referred to themselves individually as "Friends," addressed each other as "Friend," and also accepted the
designation "Quakers," bestowed on them by their rid-
iculers. The joke perpetuated by the magistrates who
mocked them was that these fervent sectarians trem-
bled, or "quaked" with anticipation as they waited for
God to speak to them directly. And they probably *did*.

I can only describe the zealous early Quakers as a
royal pain in the neck to those in authority. They re-

fused to take oaths, serve in the militia, or pay taxes to support the established church. They rejected the names of the days of the week and months of the year as pagan inventions, and they substituted numbers: first day, third month, fifth day, sixth month. They refused to doff their hats or bow in deference to magistrates or even the king because of their belief that every person was of equal worth. In an age when church and state were inseparable, Quakers refused to acknowledge the relationship. Friends also used the words "thee" and "thou" instead of "you" as a logical expression of their egalitarianism. In seventeenth-century usage, the singular pronoun "thou" was used when speaking to someone of a lower class, while the term "you" was used in conversation with equals or superiors. Quakers enthusiastically violated etiquette by using *thee, thou, thy,* and *thine* for everyone. Many were so impassioned by their newfound faith that they rushed into churches during services and urged congregants to leave "the steeplehouse" and join "the living church."

As the movement grew, persecutions of Quakers increased in England. George Fox survived eight imprisonments and several beatings, and jails were filled with hundreds of his resolute followers. Many of the early English Quakers, including my first American ancestor, Thomas "The Settler" Stokes, emigrated to the

American colonies in search of religious freedom. Yet although Quakers shared many Puritan beliefs and practices—refusal to remove their hats except for worship, an aversion to fancy dress, immoderate use of alcohol, and such "un-Godly" diversions as music, art, and theater—they suffered persecution in the New World as they had in England for their refusal to accept the majority religion. Puritans themselves had fled persecution, but that did not stop them from tyrannizing Quakers. Many were imprisoned, and between 1659 and 1661 four Quakers, one a woman, were hanged in Boston. But in states with large Quaker populations—New Jersey, Rhode Island, North Carolina, and later Pennsylvania, which was established as a Quaker colony in 1682—Quakers became accepted and often influential members of society.

The most famous Quaker of all, William Penn, was also the least likely person to become a member of this very unfashionable new sect. The son of an admiral who had aided in the restoration of King Charles II, Penn was an elegant, aristocratic young man, a charmer and an intellectual, who grew up in the highest social circles. He attended Oxford, but was expelled because of his expressions of sympathy for religious dissidents, including Quakers, whom he particularly admired. Penn became a Quaker—scandalizing his family—and in the course of two decades of writing and preaching about Quakerism in England and on the Continent suffered a number of arrests and imprisonments. But because of his own personal grace and his father's prestige, he retained his influence at court, and, despairing of religious freedom in England, successfully petitioned King Charles II to grant him a colony in America. (Since the king owed money to Admiral Penn, it was a convenient way to repay the debt.)

It was the king himself who, in 1681, gave the name Pennsylvania to the huge tract of land south of New York, west of New Jersey, and north of Maryland. The new colony, headquartered in Philadelphia, the hopefully named "City of Brotherly Love," was for Penn the fulfillment of a long-cherished vision. Penn spoke and wrote eloquently of the moral and spiritual bedrock of the new colony: full religious liberty and equality, the election by all people of a council and assembly, trial by jury, and a liberal penal system. The so-called "Holy Experiment" was the high point of Quakerism's venture into public governance.

But it was also short-lived. The pacifist Pennsylvania assembly refused to support the use of force, and dissension arose as more and more non-Quaker Pennsylvanians pushed into the western wilderness, stirred the enmity of Indians who lived there, and were unable to obtain militia protection. Other practical matters strained citizens' adherence to high ideals, and eventually Friends lost control of the state. The Holy Experiment proved once and for all time that the Quaker contribution to public life can best be made through individuals and small groups seeking to further Quaker ideals. Thereafter, Quakers confined their governance to the more intimate religious and school communities, where their special form of leadership found more natural expression.

I have always felt that the reason Quakerism took root and flourished in the colonies was because there was, and still is, something quintessentially American and profoundly democratic about this optimistic faith that declares that all people are created equal; that exalts classlessness and the perfectibility of people and institutions; that insists on the freedom to worship in whatever form one chooses—and that recognizes a direct one-to-one relationship with God.

In the nineteenth century, as the result of a schism in Quakerism, many Meetings in the midwest and western part of the country dropped the tradition of silent worship altogether and adopted a pastoral style of religious service similar to that of other Protestant denominations. They established "Quaker churches," trained "Quaker ministers," and added choirs and sermons to their worship services. But silent Meetings for Worship, the essence of Quakerism since the days of George Fox, continue to be by far the predominant form.

The traditional Quaker form of silent group worship has no parallel in other religions and has changed very little since the seventeenth century. What others call a religious "service," Friends call "Meeting for Worship," emphasizing that there is no liturgy and that worshippers come together as equal participants. But it should be noted that Quaker Meeting is not the only religious tradition of silent worship, that George Fox was not the first spiritual leader to recognize the value of silence. Siddhārtha Gautama, known today as Buddha—another young man who left his home to pursue truth—discovered silent meditation as the route to enlightenment more than two thousand years before George Fox received his message from God. But Quakers are unique in their appreciation of the spiritual power of *group* silence. If all forms of worship are attempts to transcend the self and find the divine within, Quaker Meeting uses shared silence as a medium of group discovery, as a way of sharing ourselves with others—and with God.

Quakerism is a very pragmatic religion, based on experience, not ideology. Silence is valued by Quakers because it is useful. The practice of silence—and it does take practice—is rewarding because it enriches and clarifies our lives while offering a bit of a time-out for our souls. Despite early restlessness at Quaker Meeting—I was taken each Sunday, starting at age three—I managed to learn the value of silence in childhood, when many difficult skills are more easily acquired.

When I was growing up, the restorative value of silence was affirmed at home as well as in Meeting. We always, for example, "said" a Quaker grace before meals. My sister Molly and I would be noisily needling each other while our little sister Nancy played underfoot. Mother would be rattling pots and pans or moving in and out of the dining room setting the table. And then we would sit down, talking or laughing until Mother said, "Let's say grace." We would still our voices, bow our heads, and remain totally silent for perhaps half a minute. What happened in that moment? I can only say that an extraordinary calm descended on the family. It was a moment I waited for, that I anticipated each evening with pleasure—a span of silence that invariably yielded an intense feeling of refreshment. I have found ever since that if I'm at a meal where a moment of silence before eating is not observed, I feel cheated of that small island of peace.

A highlight of my memory of boyhood is the time

I spent with my grandfather as we played chess in almost total silence. He taught me the rudiments of the game when I was very young, and as I grew up I often walked across the street to his house to play a game or two.

During those quiet times in his living room, I learned to make the best moves I could, although he regularly beat me. Sometimes he'd go over a few of our final moves to show me some options I might have considered. I recognize now that I was learning more than chess. Grandfather was trying to give my mind a framework for life, teaching me that we can move in many directions. As we sat staring at the board, silently planning our moves, he was also teaching me that we have options in life as in chess—some better than others—and that, in many instances, we must deal with situations set up by others.

My daughter Susie has a favorite recollection of the pleasures of silence during our family vacations in Maine. Each August when she and Katie and Geoff were growing up, we rented the same rambling old cottage on the shore of a small lake. There were no other houses closer than half a mile, and whatever noises we heard came from wind, water, birds, and our own voices. Eliza and I loved to sit at night or on rainy days and read for hours in the cozy, slightly musty living room. And the kids did, too. Often, after morning and afternoon swims, a long walk, and a trip to town for groceries, the five of us would gather with our books in the wicker chairs that circled the fireplace. Susie looks back on that scene as one of her happiest, most secure memories of family life. There we were, with no sound except the hiss and cracking of burning wood in the fireplace, drawing nurture from each other, even as we were each drawing sustenance from our own private thoughts.

Silence is as common as the air we breathe. It is a vast pool always available to us where we can refresh and renew ourselves, or simply stop in for a while. Silence is God's gift to our minds, a gift that modern life seems to have lost or crowded out. We need more silence in our lives, more stillness in our homes. We need, in our increasingly complex and frenetic world, to silence ourselves—and to listen.

You don't have to be a Quaker to appreciate the gift of silence. The profound Quaker concept of shared silence is gaining recognition in an age dominated by chatter. Increasingly, a moment of silence is observed before family and public events by people of varied religious backgrounds. And out of the cleansing silence, so much begins.

Friends view silence as a highly accessible treasure;

its benefits are unquestioned. The riches silence offers are available to anyone at any age and in any place. For some, the contemplative zone of silence is the morning shower, where every extraneous sound and thought is blotted out by the rush of water. For others, it is the solitary morning commute, with the steady drone of traffic outside. The key ingredient is not so much the total absence of noise as receptivity and access to the "still small voice within."

The cultivated ability to hear that voice is the most enduring value of silence. In silence we can discover the divine within, which is universally accessible but speaks to each of us in a unique voice. If we can locate, at the very center of silence, our individual "still small voice," we will have found our greatest ally in life. Because if we listen to that voice with an open heart, it will guide us through the most challenging crossroads of our lives: in work, in love, in distinguishing right from wrong.

We need only trust the voice that speaks to us out of the silence.

CHAPTER TWO

WORSHIP

QUAKERISM IS THE ONLY FAITH that is most commonly explained in a cascade of negatives. Quakerism has no theology, no body of religious dogma, no sacred books, no written creed. Traditional Quaker worship does not involve a minister, priest, or other religious leader. There is no liturgy. There are no crucifixes or other religious images in Quaker Meetinghouses or homes.

Quakers do not accept the idea of original sin, nor do they believe in a personal God who rewards and punishes. Friends do not baptize, and their wedding service is a simple exchange of vows between bride and groom within a Meeting for Worship. Despite their Christian roots and the continued interest of many Quakers in the lessons of the Gospels, the relationship between the sufferings of Christ on the cross and what Quakers call "the light within" has always been pretty murky. Forget eternal damnation. Forget salvation. And also hell, heaven, and purgatory. Look for truth within yourself and within the Meeting for Worship. Live a life of simplicity, love, and service. Let your life speak, and trust that your children will learn by your example.

The term "Meeting" is used by Friends to designate their place of worship as well as the worship service itself. As Meeting begins, worshippers walk silently into the Meetinghouse or some other designated room, or they may join at an appointed gathering place out-of-doors—Meeting can be held anywhere. They take their places on spare, wooden benches and remain seated in silence, often casting their eyes downward or closing them to "center" themselves. Because Friends believe that each individual has access to God through the powerful illumination of the light within, they worship in silence, joined in waiting for God to speak to them directly and move them to vocal ministry. If that happens, individuals stand up and deliver their message aloud. One person's message may move another to rise and, after a period of silence, another. But it is not unusual for a Meeting to be entirely silent.

At the end of approximately an hour, the person sitting at the "head" of the Meeting shakes hands with the person seated next to him. All members then lift their heads, clasp hands with those nearby, and the Meeting for Worship is concluded. This silent transfer of focus from heart to hand represents the shift at the end of Meeting from inner reflection to reconnection with the outside world. Heart and hand are the two inseparable agents of faith and work that reflect the two sides of Quakerism: its mysticism (reaching within for truth) and its activism (reaching out to others).

After Meeting, even one in which no one speaks, people emerge feeling centered and cleansed, refreshed by their hour of contemplative silence. Yet it is often difficult for people of other religions to understand that Quakers feel as spiritually uplifted after silent Meeting as non-Quakers do when they emerge from church pondering the minister's sermon and humming "Amazing Grace."

As I grew older I learned more about other religions. My non-Quaker classmates went to churches and synagogues where they listened to prayers read aloud, joined in responsively, sang joyously, and drew insight from their religious leader's sermon. Their houses of worship were handsomely decorated with crucifixes, statuary, depictions of biblical scenes on stained-glass windows. Whenever I attended one of their services, there was a whole lot to look at and listen to, and I found it fascinating and often inspiring. But in religious terms, it was like another country.

Quaker Meeting is, in the most basic sense, a group

search for truth. Quakers refer to the gradual emergence of the path to truth as "continuing revelation," a process reflected in Meeting and in every aspect of life. The premise of Quaker Meeting is that no one person sees the entire truth. The group search after truth is more comprehensive and more exacting than the search of one individual. At Meetings for Worship, the shared silence creates receptivity to the continuing revelation of the truth. People who are moved to vocal ministry offer small insights that contribute to each person's understanding.

Messages delivered by members who rise to speak at Meeting can start with any subject, but they usually end on a spiritual note within the speaker's "center" and close to the centers of other people. Plain speech and a message that everyone can understand is valued more than florid language. I was recently at a Meeting where, after about ten minutes of silence, a man rose slowly from his seat. He described a difficult experience at work, where he had tried to do something helpful but was misunderstood and made a mess of things. He said that it had really bothered him all week, but looking back, he felt this was pretty much the way things go for most of us. "We never do quite as well or as much good as we want to, even using all the 'light' as we are given," he said. "The darkness in which we so often find ourselves reminds us to constantly look for and find our way back to the light." He closed with the simple biblical injunction, "Seek and ye shall find." He was the only person who spoke that morning.

Of course, not every notion that pops into a worshipper's head during Meeting performs the elevated function of advancing the group's search for truth. Everyone who attends Meeting regularly recalls squirming while a particularly inappropriate intimacy was shared or a lengthy harangue delivered. An esteemed early Quaker, Isaac Pennington, wrote sternly in the seventeenth century of the necessity for distinguishing between thoughts suitable for vocal ministry and those "that should be kept for bread at home." There are mechanisms for dealing with people unable to perceive the distinction. A senior member of the Meeting may "elder" the speaker by interrupting with "Friend, please bring thy message to a conclusion." In extreme circumstances, a number of people may simply rise in opprobrious silence.

Each Meeting for Worship provides the setting— other people, silence, absence of distraction—that enables Quakers to receive and share flashes of illumination, to let the still inner voice of God speak to them out of the silence. I know that whatever wisdom derives from my own modest source of inner light springs directly from a chain of Meetings that stretches unbroken back to my childhood.

My first house of worship, the Moorestown Quaker Meetinghouse, was a typically simple, un-adorned building furnished with plain wooden benches. Like other Quaker Meetinghouses, it had no steeple without, no decoration within. The Meeting-house and the intimate little community in which I was born in the mid-1920s would have been recogniz-able in many ways to my ancestors. The seventeenth-century Stokeses converted to Quakerism during George Fox's evangelical ramblings through England, fled persecution, and landed in 1677 on the shores of Rancocas Creek near Burlington, New Jersey. Two and a half centuries later, I was born twelve miles from that spot in the small town of Moorestown, New Jer-sey, population five thousand, which had been, since its founding, a predominantly Quaker town. My fa-ther's ancestors had also arrived near Burlington during the same decade. Members of my extended family lived close to each other and were in constant com-munication. And almost everyone attended first day Meeting, and fifth day Meeting as well.

First day, or Sunday, Meeting was the cornerstone of life in Moorestown. Grandfather Stokes, a country doctor who had treated virtually everyone in town and had brought half of them into the world, sat at the head of the Meeting. After about an hour, it was his handshake that "broke," or ended the Meeting. As a very young child I always sat between my parents, who wanted to separate me from my sister Molly and prevent us from poking and trying to make each other laugh during the long silences. Our family sat near the back of Meeting so that Mother could quickly spirit us out if necessary. As a child, I was acutely aware that there was nothing to look at, and that most of the time nothing seemed to be *happening*.

What was happening, I came to understand, was something akin to a spiritual potluck. Each person brought something personal, simple, and sacred to the table in the belief that out of the silence, the voice of truth might be heard.

Nearly every Sunday an event occurred that remains vivid in my memory. Out of the deep, worshipful silence in which I was nearly beside myself with restlessness, a wooden bench would begin to creak. Its sound, which seemed to go on for an inordinate length of time, filled the large, spare Meeting room. Grandmother Stokes, who like other members of her Emlen family had a round, smiling face and an extraordinarily ample body, was ponderously shifting her position on the old wooden bench, preparing to get down on her sturdy knees to offer a prayer. The sound of the creaking bench riveted my wandering mind like the crack of the bat in baseball. Her voice was trembly, her spiritual vision clear, her heart uplifted and uplifting. She was always brief, and her message went something like this: "Dearly beloved Friends. Let us pray." Then there would be a meaningful pause. "Our heavenly father, help guide our hands and hearts that we may be true to thee and thy heavenly goodness to us. We ask this in thy name. Amen."

When she was finished, the room filled once more with the creaking of Grandmother's bench as she settled her massive posterior. And then all was silent again. (Kneeling to offer a prayer during Quaker Meeting was conventional in my childhood, but today, although it could happen, it would be considered odd.)

There were other members of our Meeting who spoke often and whose manner of speaking captured my attention. William Bacon Evans, known to all as "a plain Friend," always wore old-fashioned nineteenth-century Quaker garb—a plain gray suit with a jacket that buttoned up to his chin and a high hat. He had a very red face, and when he rose to speak he would stand straight, then lean a little forward and look out at everyone quietly for a minute or more until he felt ready to begin. He always spoke elliptically, as if he was leading his listeners through deep spiritual waters.

Another man who usually felt moved to speak was Master William Overman, whose title referred to his earlier post as headmaster of Moorestown Friends School. "Master William" was a white-haired, portly man, quite full of himself for a Quaker. When he rose to speak, he gripped the railing in front of him with purposeful tenacity and peered out through narrowed eyes at his fellow Quakers as if he were looking for the dawn's early light. That was when I would hear Dad's very quiet groan and see him recross his legs. Master William spoke in a voice that shook with emotion, that rose and fell in great waves, almost like singing, in the style of the early Quakers. As he spoke, his body was in perpetual motion. Molly and I were riveted by the way he swayed forward, out over the railing, and then backward in a pendulum movement that was completely in sync with his sing-song voice. As he dramatically exhorted all members of the Meeting to reach toward a higher level of living and thinking, Dad would cross and recross his legs, Molly would look around at me and make a face, or try to get her leg past Mother's and kick at me, as I slumped ingloriously down on the bench.

There were other memorable Friends in our Moorestown Meeting. Two women from the prominent British Quaker family of chocolate manufacturers, the Cadburys, were valued members. One, who had been in charge of the American Friends Service Committee's work in Vienna after World War II, always had something interesting and worldly to contribute. My mother often said that she had "a beautiful spirit."

Traditional Quaker Meeting, as inaugurated in the seventeenth century, has been called an experiment in religious anarchy. Because all authority is vested in all members, all people are equally entitled to speak. Each Meeting is like a gamble with the human spirit, a wager that more will be brought out of the room than was brought in—more depth, more insight, more truth, more knowledge, more growth in each and among all. An individual's "vocal ministry" is expected to conform to the ideal of sharing the light within as a means of reaching the light in others. It should also be both succinct and spontaneous. But it doesn't always happen that way.

I should know. When I was headmaster at Sidwell Friends School in Washington, D.C., I used to think in advance of the weekly school Meetings about the message I might deliver. A gross, un-Quakerly gambit. But school Meetings were very special, the one time in the week when I had the opportunity to say something that I hoped students and teachers would reflect on deeply while sitting together, the separations of age and station obliterated in the silence. Often it was simply a line from a poem or an excerpt from something I'd been reading that gave me—and them, I hoped—something to ponder. In thinking about what to say, I always had in mind a classic prescription of my favorite teacher at Columbia University graduate school, Mark Van Doren. Van Doren often said that what matters most is not what you think about something but "the best that can be thought about it." A search for the best that can be thought as we look within ourselves is, I believe, what should move us to speak at Meeting—and, as much as possible, in daily life. What we find within us in deep thought or in silent listening is, I would hold, truth.

All Meetings are different. At some, quoting from the Gospels is commonplace. In others, most messages draw a relationship between an event in everyday life and a shared moral or social concern. Friends in large urban and suburban areas that offer several options often shop around before joining a Meeting that suits their tastes. One Meeting might seem to them more spiritual. One more action oriented. Does this Meeting have many young converts? Is that one particularly welcoming to gay and lesbian members? Does another have members whose "ministry" is consistently meaningful? Or does it tend to have "popcorn" meetings, where men and women—often riled up about a current issue or an article they read in the morning paper—keep "popping up" with messages that are political rather than spiritual?

But for all their differences, Meetings for Worship are fundamentally the same. At each Meeting, a group of individuals gathers and, open to the word of God, waits in attentive, expectant silence for a spark of the divine in their midst. Sometimes it comes in words; sometimes in silence. The language of truth can often be heard in silence, if only we know how to listen.

Ernest Hemingway wrote, "If you are lucky enough to have lived in Paris as a young man, then wherever you go for the rest of your life, it stays with you, for Paris is a moveable feast." I feel the same way about Meeting; it is a moveable feast of the spirit. No matter where you worship, or who joins you in your silent search, the truth is always waiting there for you like an old friend.

IF WE HOPE TO BE GUIDED by an inner light, by an inner voice of truth, how do we distinguish this "true" voice among the internal chorus that calls out to us—the voices of self-interest, of vanity, of selfish pleasure?

If a man feels compelled to leave his wife and children to pursue a personal vision of fulfillment, is this the voice of truth calling to him? If a person is infatuated with the pleasures of food, drink, and gambling and devotes most of his waking hours and disposable income to these pursuits, is this his true nature speaking?

The answer, I believe, lies in George Fox's sublimely optimistic vision of human nature. If there is that of God in every person, then truth is the *best* that there is in each of us—the part of us that is naturally drawn toward the good, toward God. If we listen for the truth—for the best that is within us—then our lives will begin to "speak" the truth. As George Fox said,

CHAPTER THREE

TRUTH

"Truth comes from within. It is the basis for daily life, like the food we eat."

Our most readily available tool for distinguishing truth in our daily lives is common sense. Like truth, common sense may be hard to define—but we recognize it when we see it. We call it "common" because it's shared by all. In the same way that we know the difference between right and wrong, between good and evil, we are each endowed with the capacity to apprehend the truth—about ourselves and about the world around us.

As self-proclaimed "Publishers of the Truth," seventeenth-century Friends announced to all who would listen, "The truth is the way, and the way is the truth." And this focus on truth, in all its aspects, has remained central to Quaker worship and Quaker life. Truth, Quakers believe, restores our souls and empowers our actions. Truth is our guide, and truth is our liberator. Quakers often quote the apostle John, who condensed the message eloquently when he proclaimed, "The truth shall set you free."

It's a radical concept, but Quakers have always embraced it as reality: The truth *will* make us free—free from meaninglessness, free from lovelessness, free from the emptiness and frustrations of egocentricity.

The search for truth is central to a meaningful life,

but it is not as simple as adhering to a prescribed ideology. Each Quaker Meeting involves everyone who
attends in a search for truth, and belief in vocal ministry
as a counterpart to silent worship and as an instrument
of continuing revelation remains basic to Quakerism.
Friends hold that one can find truth and new insights
at each Meeting for Worship, each Meeting for Business—held monthly to address practical concerns rang-
ing from repairing the Meetinghouse roof to drafting a
letter of protest to a congressman to Meeting finances—
and in life generally. It is an interactive process that
requires openness, diligence, and discipline in equal
measure. The search for truth is a lifelong pact with our
inner lives that encompasses seeking the truth, recognizing the truth, speaking the truth, and living the
truth—which is to say, letting our lives speak.

Quakers also search for truth through a device
known as the "query." Queries, such as "Do we really
observe simplicity and honesty in everyday life?" or
"Are love and harmony within the Meeting community fostered by a spirit of sharing?" are designed to
prick the conscience and prompt both group and individual self-examination. A query is like a burr under
the saddle of the soul. Although queries have varied
through time and from one area of the country to an-

other, they invariably focus on helping Meetings and individual Friends conduct their spiritual and temporal lives in accordance with their religious beliefs. Specific queries may be revisited from time to time within a Quaker community, evoking quite different responses.

Meetings for Business are conducted in the same spirit as Meetings for Worship. In fact, these Meetings are routinely referred to as "a Meeting for Worship with a concern for business." Many Meetings for Business begin with the reading of queries such as: "Are Meetings for Business held in a spirit of worship, understanding, and forbearance? Is the Meeting aware that it speaks not only through its actions but also through its failure to act?"

Following the reading of the query, there is usually a substantial period of silence. The clerk then shuffles his or her papers, signifying it's time to take up the Meeting's business. Quakers come to Meeting for Business not to promote an opinion but to join in the search for truth. The goal is to build "clearness" around the matter at hand. Decisions and actions take place when the group's discussion has resulted in a "sense of the Meeting," when the clerk, with careful and sensitive discernment, finds that the Meeting is "clear" about the matter at hand.

This nonvoting process is often slow, but Quakers believe that clearness can be found in the group's patient search for answers, through careful listening, and through speaking from the heart. In reaching a sense of the Meeting, everyone present shares in the result. For Friends, the *process* of reaching a decision is as important as the decision itself. When very contentious subjects are being discussed, and vehement disagreements arise, the clerk may ask for a period of silence, which can become quite lengthy, to give people a chance to "seek divine guidance" and try to see the subject in a new way.

Many of the subjects discussed are not nearly as weighty as this description might indicate. A question addressed periodically at my Meeting, for example, is whether young children should attend the first fifteen minutes of Meeting or the last. The Religious Education Committee has recommended the former course, but after considerable discussion it has become clear that there is no "sense of the Meeting" about which would serve the children's and the Meeting's interests best. So the subject is carried over to the next Meeting for Business and the next, and will continue to be discussed until the sense of the Meeting is reached.

The collective search after truth as practiced in Meeting for Worship and Meeting for Business flies in the face of the more romantic vision of an individual's solitary search. But the individual and the group search are not mutually exclusive, because the search for truth is not restricted to Meeting. Every day of our lives is another journey down the path of truth. We cannot withdraw from the process of living while we make up our minds how to live. All we can do is move forward, guided by whatever inner light we can find to show us the way.

Quakers believe that if "The truth is the way, and the way is the truth," then a key to finding one's "way" in the world is the deceptively simple act of speaking the truth. We live, however, in a society where it is virtually taken for granted that many of the people we listen to are not telling the truth. We distrust the words of politicians, businesspeople, the press, advertisers, you name it. Most public discourse is suffocated by rhetoric in the service of an effect and argumentation that insults thought in the service of a chosen conclusion. Facts and truth often seem to be incidental and accidental.

In this climate of cynicism, how can we embrace the Quaker message that, despite the complexity of modern life, we must be true to our best selves? How shall we act on information that we suspect is not true?

How do we teach our children the importance of integrity, and also arm them against blind acceptance of false claims and information?

The question might reasonably be asked: What is the value of truth-telling and why should we bother to continue to teach it to our children? Is telling the truth, after all, just a quaint anachronism that has outlived its usefulness? No. Not at all. Friends are practical people, and when they speak of truth-telling, they are referring to a concept that has profound pragmatic implications. Think of truthful speech as the bridge between the silent search after truth and letting your life speak. If you speak the truth, you will be true to yourself, to that which is best in you. Speaking the truth is the first step toward letting your life speak in a way that is honest and authentic.

Speaking the truth is so central to Quaker belief that Quakers have always refused to take oaths. Since they are expected to tell the truth at all times, they reject the idea that there are two standards of truth—one for everyday concerns and one for the courtroom. There are many stories about the reluctance of Friends to shade the truth in any way. One is about a farmer who walked down the road and saw a shorn sheep in a field. When asked if the sheep he saw was shorn he replied, "Well, certainly he was shorn on the side facing the road." Others concern the more significant matter of Quakers who participated in the Underground Railroad. When asked if any runaway slaves were being sheltered on his property, a Friend did not lie when he replied, "There are no slaves here," because it was his belief that no human being could be a slave. Other Quakers brought food and money to runaway slaves in total darkness, so that if they were asked whether they'd seen any runaway Negroes, they could truthfully respond in the negative.

I had a cousin who used to reply regularly to the casual comment "That's funny" with an emphatic "It's not funny at all," thus carrying Quaker honesty to absurd lengths. I'm afraid I must add that many Quakers have underdeveloped senses of humor.

Friends do not take pride in the second Quaker president, Richard Nixon. Herbert Hoover, the first Quaker president, attended the Friends Meeting of Washington. Nixon never showed up. That's the least of it. What horrified and continues to bring shame on his co-religionists—whether they be Republicans, Democrats, liberals, conservatives—has less to do with Nixon's domestic or foreign policy or actions than with the unarguable fact that he did not tell the truth.

Plato told us more than two thousand years ago, "Truth is the beginning of every good thing, both in

Heaven and on earth; and he who would be blessed and happy should be from the first a partaker of truth, for then he can be trusted."

The prick of conscience that comes with the violation of truth is a reminder that integrity is the first principle in life, a principle all of us want to instill in our children—not only out of some vague sense of morality but for the most practical reasons as well. Our ability to trust one another—in love, in business, in every arena of life—can only be based on a mutual commitment to honesty.

Experience has taught me that, quite aside from high-flown issues of morality, truth-telling simplifies life. Again, the litmus test of pragmatism. The person who makes a practice of telling the truth does not need to confront each small situation with the question: Shall I speak truth? Shall I say I bought something in this store and get them to stamp my parking ticket? Shall I say I have the flu and spend the day at the ballpark instead of the office?

Lying burdens and complicates life. It gets us into trouble. It undermines relationships. And lies can be hard to remember. The questions "What did I say to her about it?" "What reason did I give when I told him I wasn't coming in to work?" "What excuse did I give for not going to her party?" do not trouble or confuse people who consistently tell the truth. If we are resolved to tell the truth, even when it is inconvenient to do so, we are relieved of a guilty conscience and the fear of being found out. Telling the truth simply feels better.

And yet, making a commitment to truth is frightening to many people. We fear exposing ourselves to others. We are afraid that our truth-telling will make people angry or lay us open to ridicule. If we can no longer hide behind falsehoods, then we must live with the truth—which can indeed appear as an unsettling alternative. What happens if I can't make up false excuses for not doing what I don't want to do? What happens if I can't cover up my actions with a "little white lie"?

I would make the case for taking the apostle John's teaching literally—the truth *can* set us free. There is nothing so liberating as simply speaking the truth from your heart, nothing so empowering as believing in what you say—and in having others perceive you as truthful. Think how much we all respect and value the honest opinion of our closest friends and confidants. Consider how hungry we all are for public figures who dare to tell the truth and act on their own true beliefs. It takes courage to tell the truth, and when one person makes that leap of faith, it gives strength to all of us.

Having said all this, truth-telling inevitably presents its own dilemmas. I realize that it's difficult to be dogmatic about truth-telling because, in some instances, telling the whole truth and nothing but the truth can be ruthless, unfeeling, and destructive. Truth is like the north star: It points the way. But Quakers often discover an incompatibility between two compelling beliefs: that we should unswervingly tell the truth and that we should always love others.

The problem with speaking out totally truthfully in a family is that it so often conflicts with love. Telling a fragile and frightened spouse or parent every detail of the doctor's dire news, for instance, is not the sort of truth-telling that is helpful to anyone. Telling a child who enjoys playing the piano that she hasn't much talent is hurtful and destructive. And if your host asks if you enjoyed the dinner, the answer is always yes. It's been said that if everyone blurted out the truth about everyone else, there wouldn't be two friends left in the world.

Speaking your true feelings in a close working community can also be counterproductive. In the 1960s there was a strong sense among some younger faculty members at Sidwell Friends School, where I was headmaster, that there should be no dissembling in faculty meetings, that everyone should be absolutely truthful about his or her feelings even if that meant speaking insensitively to a colleague. If the collegiality they observed was dependent on hypocrisy, they believed, it was essentially dishonest. In fact, their in-your-face candor was so disturbing to longtime faculty members—who found it so un-Quakerly!—that some of the senior teachers stopped participating in faculty meetings. I found I needed to vigorously defend civility and remind my truth-at-all-costs colleagues that, as we often told the students, the important thing is to put the group first. Only by being supportive of one another can we learn to work together. One of the paradoxes of running a Quaker school is that expression of individual conviction lies at the heart of Quakerism, and yet the good of the school cannot be sacrificed to any one individual's convictions, however deeply held.

In speaking the truth, there are no absolutes, no perfect answers. My personal rule is to tell the truth unless doing so is likely to cause serious harm. I find this one of the easiest rules to adhere to. If we aspire to be true to ourselves, we must know our personal boundaries, and maintaining a code of truth-telling is a good start. The philosopher Immanuel Kant said that in regard to truth-telling, we should be more forgiving of others' shortcomings and more demanding of our own. But whatever our personal rules may be, they remain individual parameters that only we can draw.

What does this mean in our daily lives, lives in which we're confronted with a host of decisions that may lead to the most trivial or the most grave consequences?

Recently a woman asked my advice about a situation that had led her to some painful self-examination. The action that worried her was trivial, but the implications troubled her conscience. On a recent birthday her mother-in-law gave her a bottle of perfume, a gift she received in the presence of her young daughter with a false demonstration of enthusiasm since it was a scent she was familiar with and didn't particularly like.

A week later she decided to use the expensive fragrance as a gift for a woman she and her daughter were visiting with overnight in another city. She warned her daughter not to mention to their hostess that it had been given to her by Grandma. She explained that, in fact, she had more perfume than she could use—something Grandma couldn't have known—and that her friend liked this particular scent. When the friend opened the gift and thanked her warmly, the little girl shot her mother a look of sly complicity. And the mother felt a strong pang of uneasiness.

"You're a Quaker," she said to me, "and I know Quakers always tell the truth. Did I really do something terribly wrong, or is this harmless sort of lying okay?"

The fact that she asked the question indicated that her conscience had already given her the answer and that some harm had resulted. The simple and consoling response from me would have been that no one was injured by her deception, the friend would enjoy the gift, and her mother-in-law would never find out or suffer hurt feelings. But another consequence of her action was that she was implicitly teaching her daughter, by example, that Mom considered lying "okay."

The Quaker message to my grandchildren who will grow up in wonder and delight and only slowly discover that the world is indifferent and often hostile to their expectations and dreams is this:

Life is not a problem that can be solved. It must be lived each day, and each day brings a jumble of choices that challenge our practical wisdom, our common sense, and our yearning for truth. Your choices in life are enormous. They come at you in battalions. You've been learning from the cradle that it's important to be good at something—math, music, spelling, sports. Remember also to pay attention to the spirit's first command—to be good at life.

Truth seems to speak to us continually and insistently through our conscience. But we also hear other messages from deep within, and one of the most urgent is to be true to yourself, to be you. Growing up, I was very good at figuring out what kind of person others expected me to be, and sometimes these expectations were the opposite of who I really was. Sometimes I still feel as if my life is a struggle between these two me's. I think this ongoing contest for my soul helps keep me, in some strange way, morally fit, that the conflict is something God intended when He made us "a little lower than the angels," creatures who must contend with all the conflicts in our nature, at the core of which is truth.

The best way to discover truth is to pay attention to our hearts. Life experiences—particularly our own sufferings and those of people closest to us—exercise our hearts, and increase our wisdom. "The heart," wrote the French philosopher René Pascal, "has its reasons, which reason knows nothing of." The search for truth is equally available to all people. Living in each of us is a seed of the divine, an inner light of truth. Although it's there, we must turn toward this light and acknowledge its power to illuminate our path. All we need is simplicity of spirit, silence, and an atmosphere in which to center down without distraction. Think of it as the same light that has guided people like you throughout the ages. We cannot be true to anything if we are not true to ourselves, to our inner light. Quakers like to spell the noun "truth" with a capital "T" to emphasize its significance. Yet they also believe that truth merely as a concept is powerless; it has relevance only when the word is married to deeds.

Remember that when we speak about truth, we're not talking about mathematical truth; we're talking about knowledge that we can only find for ourselves. Our lives are so busy that it's difficult for us to take the time to seek truth. We're too engaged in keeping up, getting by, moving through the daily routine and amusing ourselves. But reminders can come at any moment during the day. Something in you says—*Wait a second: Is this the me I want to be?*—and during that momentary illumination you will find your answer.

The poet Walt Whitman astutely defined truth as "Whatever satisfies the soul." The query "What satisfies the soul?" can help us distinguish things we truly desire from those that merely attract us. We can be attracted to and stimulated by many things. By power. By beauty. By things that are new and different. But our soul is only satisfied, our spirits only nourished, by the truth.

CHAPTER FOUR

SIMPLICITY

THE MOST VALUABLE ASPECT of religion is that it provides us with a framework for living. I have always felt that the beauty and power of Quakerism is that it exhorts us to live more truthfully, more simply, more charitably. For many Friends, simplicity is a cornerstone of their faith that continues to define their daily lives.

For Quakers, simplicity is truth's twin virtue: The two concepts are seamlessly intertwined. Without simplicity of spirit, we are not prepared to receive the truth. And if we fail to act in accordance with the truth, we cannot let our lives speak. Yet I fear that the Quaker concept of simplicity is commonly misunderstood. The simplicity of lifestyle that Friends extol is not based on forsaking worldly goods and pursuing some vision of a less complex bygone era. It's more like a reliable standard that is always available, a first cousin of moderation that can become a way of life. Living simply is also not about finding a quiet corner where you can contemplate your life and feel good about yourself. Far from it. It's about giving yourself the freedom to pursue that indestructible impulse to do good in the world, to go toward the best.

Quakers are not the only people who have extolled simplicity—Henry David Thoreau called out for the simple life with an austerity few Quakers ever envisioned—but for Quakers this concept is directly related to basic religious beliefs and observances. A person who is preoccupied with materialistic desires is ill prepared to sit in silence with other worshippers and listen for the still small voice of God.

Quakers do not categorize the sacred and the secular as separate realms. For Friends the word "simplicity" describes a way of life that follows naturally from a way of worshipping. All you need for worship is a quiet place or a plain Meetinghouse. All you need to share the light within and help find truth is plain, clear language among seekers. All you need for living are a few possessions, simplicity of spirit, and readiness to answer to the divine spark in every person.

You certainly don't have to be a Quaker to strive for a simpler life, but it helps. For Quakers, exposure to simplicity begins early as you sit silently in Meeting on a plain wooden bench with nothing to look at except bare walls and plain-looking people, most with their heads down. No music. Nothing to listen to at all except occasional speaking. It may be hard at first, because children are restless and easily distracted, but in this atmosphere, simplicity gradually grows on you— or perhaps I should say *in* you.

The word "simplicity" didn't get much attention from the early Quakers, who used the term "plain" because it was less abstract. They espoused "plain dress" and "plain speech," manifestations of simplicity one could see and hear. One aspect of plain speech was the use of the words "thee" and "thou" instead of "you," a custom that was in transition when I was growing up and would go out entirely in my children's generation. My two sisters and I said "you" to each other and to most—but not all—friends and cousins. But we automatically used the old terms "thee" and "thou" in even the most informal family conversation when addressing our mother, father, grandparents, aunts and uncles, and our revered Great Aunt Sally of Germantown. Though childless herself, Aunt Sally was the true matriarch of the family. White-haired and dressed in gray, she hosted large family gatherings in her big old Victorian house on Coulter Street, sitting just inside the front door to welcome each arriving family member with a delighted smile and a loving word.

Most of my relatives addressed each other in the

old Quaker style. But Dad, who seemed somehow more human than saintly—he liked sailing, beer, a pipe, conviviality, the life of the city—hardly ever used "thee" or "thou" within the family or without, although he was addressed that way by others. Years later when I left Moorestown and entered Harvard, Dad came to visit me, and I recall having a sudden anxious thought. Would I dare to address him as "thee" in front of my sophisticated college roommate and risk being judged terminally different, even quaint? When the moment arrived, the answer became obvious. It would have been unthinkable for me to address either my father or mother as "you." I realized that although I had left home for the big city and a non-Quaker college, neither the plain speech I had heard since infancy nor the values it reflected were things I could leave behind. They were an inseparable part of who I was.

Plain speech is only one aspect of the simple life. If I were asked to define Quaker simplicity in a nutshell, I would say that it has little to do with how many things you own and everything to do with not letting your possessions own you. Today, we are all weighed down by the burdens and seductions of ordinary life. We live in an age of irresistibly high-impact advertising. Television ads market hundred-dollar running shoes to children whose families haven't enough money to feed them properly. Rich and poor children alike are aroused to a frenzy of covetousness by promotions of expensive new toys. We can purchase almost anything we want immediately—with a phone call if we haven't time in our busy schedules for a trip to the store. Credit cards give us instant buying power. ATM machines give us instant cash.

"What do I need?" is simplicity's fundamental question, a question that rubs against our natural proclivity for acquiring things, a question few of us feel ready to address. America's favorite weekend activity is not participating in sports, gardening, hiking, reading, visiting with friends and neighbors. It's shopping. More often impelled by acquisitiveness than by necessity, we set out to buy or just to look and dream. We gain a false and fleeting sense of self-esteem from our ability to purchase expensive things for ourselves and our children. The vibrancy of our busy malls has made them virtual community centers. We leave boredom and emptiness behind as we browse through their glittering corridors of stuff. Yet many of us have learned that acquiring too much stuff can get in the way of happiness, that it can obscure what is best in us, lead us back to boredom and emptiness, corrupt our children's values. We often step out of the mall blinking in the sunshine at the end of an almost-vanished afternoon feeling unsatisfied, regretful, grumpy.

Many conscientious young parents find that the question of how to deal with children's marketing-induced materialism has become a central issue in their lives. How, they ask, do you decide what to give children and what to deny them? How, they wonder, do you properly balance what children need and what they want? How do you teach them not to confuse *things* with *love*?

Although the pressure to acquire is much more intense than it was when I was a child, the lust for material goods is not merely a late-twentieth-century phenomenon. I grew up with cousins in Moorestown and nearby Germantown, Pennsylvania, whose parents were infinitely more wealthy than mine. Some of the boy cousins I played with had toys and sports equipment that boggled my imagination and incited in me a quite un-Quakerly jealousy. I can still visualize in remarkable detail the treasure trove of electric trains, the pool table, and the Ping-Pong table that occupied the large basement playroom of one of my cousins.

I recently asked my grandchildren Christopher, twelve, and Jennifer, nine, what they thought it meant to be a Quaker. After considering the question briefly they agreed that "to be a Quaker means to be simple. Quakers don't need a lot of things." Although I was delighted with this response, I must add that their parents, Katie and Rick, say they often have to "debrief" their kids after they come home from playing with friends whose homes and lifestyles are considerably more affluent than their own. Some discussion of what they enjoyed at their friends' houses and gentle reminders of the family's commitment to a less materialistic way of life seem to work—at least for a while.

The Quaker response to children's zest for acquisitions is that parents must get their own priorities in order and not let superfluity interfere with the attempt to live a simple life. Parents can let their lives speak by helping their children recognize what nonmaterial things excite and engage them. Children learn much less from what they're told than from what they observe. Does the family relish dinners together at which everyone shares the events and thoughts of his and her day? Do they enjoy hiking, camping, working together on a community project? Do they think it's a lot more fun to go to a neighborhood picnic on a summer weekend afternoon than to go to the mall? Do they appear fulfilled even though they don't have an excess of stuff?

I suffered as a child from some confusion about the meaning of simplicity because I lived across the street from and was in daily communication with my Grandfather and Grandmother Stokes. Both were highly esteemed in our community for their Quaker piety, yet they lived in a style that seemed to me extraordinarily lavish. My grandparents' spacious and gracious house stood on a hill and had a huge sloping lawn that led to a delectable strawberry patch. Behind the house was a croquet lawn and a field where Grandfather's cow grazed. Grandfather bought a new Buick every three years to the month, traveled widely and often, and had three servants—a cook, a maid, and a farmer. He and Grandmother also had a cottage at Pocono Lake Preserve in Pennsylvania, a large, private tract of woods and streams surrounding a quiet lake. A small group of Quaker families had leased it at the turn of the century and preserved its rustic beauty.

Grandfather's simplicity was certainly not that of Thoreau, who warned, "Our life is frittered away by detail. Simplicity, simplicity, simplicity! I say, let your affairs be two or three and not a hundred or a thousand. Keep your accounts on your thumbnail." Although his accounts were much too extensive to keep on his thumbnail, Grandfather taught us that time and money were never to be wasted. Money was like oil. It made things go, but it was kept out of sight. It was never a subject of conversation, although he kept avid track of it in a little notebook to make it as serviceable as possible. And Grandfather's trips, money, the new Buick, croquet, strawberries, summers at the lake were all part of sharing, of passing on ideas, experience, knowledge, of exercising heart and mind for his children, grandchildren, relatives, and friends.

It wasn't until I was grown and lived away that I realized how simplicity manifested itself in my grandfather's very full and gratifying life. What I recalled with sudden insight is something that often happened after a grand Sunday dinner. Picture the family in the 1930s—my two sisters and I and Mother and Dad, sitting at the table on Sunday after Meeting with Grandfather and Grandmother, our heads bowed in silent Quaker grace. Raising his head, Grandfather broke the silence and somehow, as if by magic, the pantry door swung open and in swept Christine, the cook, with a substantial roast chicken, complete with fixings and followed by homemade ice cream and cake.

But it was the after-dinner ritual that stuck with me all my life and that symbolizes for me the true meaning of simplicity. Grandfather would often propose a drive to "the pines"—the Jersey pinelands that began about fifteen miles east of Moorestown and extended for forty miles or so to the Atlantic coast. After the main road ended, we drove more miles on bumpy curving lanes and then on sandy roads that branched off into indistinguishable side roads to who knows where, until we reached a point in the woods where the road just stopped. We then started to walk, following Grandfather to a tiny spring surrounded by rich green flora. Reaching down, Grandfather would push aside some plants to disclose a tiny yellow bloom, beautiful beyond words—the only flower of its kind around and, it turns out, one of the few in the Western world. An ardent and knowledgeable naturalist, Grandfather had discovered and identified this little yellow flower years before, and the Academy of Natural Sciences in Philadelphia had named it *Ficaria Ficaria*. How did he find it in the first place, and how did he find it again and again, season after season, among the sandy stretches of unmarked roads?

Over the years I've come to think of those sumptuous dinners followed by treks to see a virtually lost botanical marvel as a metaphor for the simplicity with which my grandfather lived and breathed. At the end of the day, it isn't the things we accumulate and that have cushioned us that count for anything. What counts is our ability to recognize the small miracles sprouting in our midst and to share them with others. What always impressed me, even as a boy, was the way my grandfather would almost explode with delight at the sight of that small yellow bloom. I'm confident his excitement had much less to do with the fact that it was his discovery than with his unbounded joy in God's creation.

Of course, I am not the first person to point out that the best things in life are free, but the traps and snares of modern life have made the pleasures that are right there in front of us harder to recognize. Simplicity gets admiring deference from many of us who think we'd like more of it in our lives—if only we could discover how it's done. If we travel in parts of Pennsylvania, Delaware, or other areas where Amish people live, we are fascinated by the sight of contemporary men and women in broad-brimmed hats and bonnets making their way down the road in a horse-drawn carriage. They seem to be in a world of their own, and we wish we knew where they were going at such a nice, easy pace, and what they were thinking about in all that slow time under those big hats. Our wonderment comes from deep within us, from a feeling that our lives too should be less cluttered, less stressful. The feeling never lasts, but it's there. We just don't give it time to take much of a hold on us. Maybe the time has come to pay it some real attention.

Simplicity, like all virtues, is valuable because it is useful. I have come to understand that making life simpler does for our minds what getting in shape does for our bodies. It makes us feel more in control, more centered, more effective. And as with getting into shape, you have to want it sincerely, and you have to work at it consciously every day.

I have found that simplicity is an indispensable ally in giving ordinary life extraordinary meaning. The French philosopher and essayist Montaigne wrote, "If you have known how to compose your life, you have accomplished a great deal more than the man who knows how to compose a book. All other things—to reign, to hoard, to build—are, at most, inconsiderable props and appendages. The great and glorious masterpiece of man is to be able to live to the point."

Simplicity helps us to live to the point, to clear the way to the best, to keep first things first.

CHAPTER FIVE

CONSCIENCE

WHEN I WAS A CHILD I didn't think about "living to the point." And no one in my protective Quaker community quoted Montaigne or, for that matter, any other thinkers. Quakers always valued life experience more than received wisdom. The prescriptive that you should always remember to act in a way that would "let your life speak" seemed to me a pretty inclusive rule of conduct.

It was clear to me from a young age that letting your life speak was more than a spiritual notion. The divine spark that Quakers believe dwells within each of us is a birthright that carries a solemn responsibility for action. "I saw," George Fox wrote in his *Journal,* "that there was an ocean of darkness and death, but also an infinite ocean of light and love, which flowed over the ocean of darkness." As a child I understood this to mean that by leading a good life and serving others we

allied ourselves with the forces of light. Good *can* overcome evil in this world, I was taught, but only if we
commit ourselves to making our lives part of the "infinite ocean of light."

Looking back I realize that my confident, unques-
tioning view of the future was rooted in the fact that I
simply, and rather simplistically, assumed that my religion would provide me with all the guidelines I needed
to become the sort of man I hoped to be. I was for-
tunate in my role models—parents, grandparents, uncles, older cousins I looked up to with admiration. All
were staunch Quakers of unquestioned integrity. When
we gathered in great noisy numbers at Aunt Sally's
home in Germantown for enormous Christmas and
New Year's Day dinners, I looked around at the joyous
assemblage of Smiths, Stokeses, Emlens, Shipleys, and
Scattergoods and felt certain that in the battle between
the forces of darkness and light, we were staunch war-
riors in the ranks of the forces of light.

In 1936, when I was only twelve, the snug and—
let's face it—smug universe I was living in began to
feel the tremors of a world at war. Hitler marched into
the Rhineland, Mussolini invaded Ethiopia, the Spanish
Civil War began, China and Japan went to war. Events
in far-off countries I knew about only from maps

would lead me to a crisis of conscience in which I recognized that my religion did not offer the easy answers I had always counted on receiving.

Within a few years I would come to grips with the question I'd never before asked myself: *What do I do if our country goes to war?*

The Quaker answer to that question was implicit in the air I breathed at home, at my grandparents' Sunday dinners, and at Meeting. There is that of God in every person, George Fox taught, and this central Quaker belief dictates that Quakers do not discriminate against, cheat, harm, or kill anyone, even in the interest of defending their country. William Penn, perhaps the most eloquent spokesman for Quakerism, also spoke out against violence. "Force subdues," he wrote, "but love gains, and he that forgives first wins the laurel."

The Quaker dictate of nonviolence was reinforced through every encounter in my close, warm world. It was a message I had been absorbing all my life—easy to learn and easy to believe. The directive from Fox, from Penn, from Smiths and Stokeses and Emlens was to love your fellowman and do good. And in 1936 this seemed, without question, to preclude shooting rifles and tossing grenades.

Eight years later I was a private in an infantry com-

pany, marching through the snowy Belgian woods toward the Battle of the Bulge.

We moved slowly through the early morning, walking in single columns on opposite sides of a tree-lined country road. It was cold and clear with patches of snow on the ground. After walking in silence for nearly an hour, we came around a sharp curve and confronted a terrifying sight—an immense German tank sunk partway in the ditch, its 88-millimeter cannon pointing to the sky. We'd heard about Tiger tanks, the biggest and deadliest of all armored weapons, but this was the first one I'd seen up close. There it was, seventy-five tons of cold brown steel. Stark and ugly and mechanical and inhuman—like a huge predatory animal, even in its destroyed state. After a month of following in the wake of other people's battles, we knew our war had begun.

We made no sound as we passed by the behemoth, awed, half expecting it to come alive and strike out at us. We continued down the road through the silent snow-filled woods, when suddenly our company was strafed and bombed by our own P-38s, which mistook us for disguised Germans who had been raising havoc on parts of the front. I swan-dived into the ditch as machine-gun bullets dug a deadly line down the middle of the narrow dirt road. Then I and the others who had sheltered there scrambled out of the ditch and crawled, scared out of our wits, into the woods, hoping to escape the bombs that were still falling. I never found out how many men were lost in those two or three minutes, but there were bodies and cries and moans all around.

Early the next morning three of us were picked to carry machine-gun ammunition through a wooded area thinly held by the Germans to a front-line company holding a ridge above the Belgian town of Grandmenil. As we plodded through the snow with our heavy loads, we began passing dead Germans. Here was the enemy in the flesh. We stared at the wasted bodies of young men who looked very much like us. By dumb luck we avoided being hit by sniper and mortar fire that day. I escaped with only a cut on the top of my left hand, and I can still see the scar in dim outline as I write these words.

Later that day Grandmenil was abandoned. As we walked in to town, we were assaulted by the stench of dead Germans piled in a corn crib. We gazed in awe at the bombed-out houses, the church with its steeple sheared away and huge holes in all its sides, and the dead horses lying stiffly on their backs, their legs like short black trees rising out of bloated black bodies. There was debris of every description everywhere. And heavy silence.

How far is it from Moorestown to Grandmenil?

As far as the moon to my Quaker friends. Yet for me they were inseparable, joined firmly in the part of the mind where conscience meets relentless reality. Somehow, in my Quaker youth I had failed to grasp one of my religion's basic messages—that the God within you, the still small voice, is what tells you right from wrong. Not parents. Not teachers. Not wise men and women writing in books. George Fox made it clear that each Friend should be free to "follow the light." Since Friends always emphasized personal experience rather than reliance on authority, "following the light" can be more concretely described as following your individual conscience.

My personal path to Grandmenil began in early August 1941 when I was seventeen and enjoying a two-week canoe trip down the Allegash River through the northern Maine woods with some fellow campers. The sound of water flowing over rocks suddenly gave way to an enormous roar as multiple formations of large warplanes appeared overhead, flying northeast toward Canada and the Atlantic as part of Roosevelt's Lend-Lease to England "in its darkest hour." They were out of sight and hearing in less than half a minute, but in those few seconds our sheltered world was transformed into a place under the control of ominous, far-off events.

Through the years that scene has remained a vivid metaphor for a great deal of what I've learned about life: its unpredictability, its relentless refusal to exclude evil even from what's best and most precious, its inscrutable and insensate control over the best of plans and hopes. I also remember the sound of those warplanes as the first alarms of conscience in my life—a startling new experience.

When I arrived home and told Mother and Dad about this event they seemed reluctant to discuss the war. What they really wanted to talk about was where I'd be applying for college. I knew their views on the subject reflected their fears and convictions about the momentous draft question. The choices were Haverford, the Quaker college that Dad and a great many relatives had attended and where my cousins would be going, and Harvard, which had always seemed to me an alluring option. Mother was sure that if I chose Haverford I'd be surrounded by students whose views would reinforce all the things I'd learned growing up, and I'd decide to be a conscientious objector.

Dad's views were far less opaque. He had served in

World War I in the Medical Corps in France, frustrated at being behind the front lines. Every so often a boisterous army buddy of Dad's named Garrett came for Sunday supper. Dad enjoyed hearing him brag about his frontline exploits and thought, I suspect, that it would be good for me to absorb the memories of a real veteran—one who had been gassed and whose head had a "tick." Mother tolerated these episodes but always emphasized to me after Garrett had left that he was "a little bit off." Despite Mother's fears, Garrett's tales of a war that seemed long ago had little influence on me. What was becoming increasingly obvious to me was that Hitler was a brutal murderer who must be opposed, and that fascism was the closest thing to an ocean of darkness that I was likely to encounter in this life.

Is there that of God in every man? Can you maintain that ideal in a world dominated by barbaric cruelty? Doesn't keeping humanity alive take precedence over belief in nonviolence? These were the questions posed by the inner voice I began to hear—and heed. All these thoughts plus less weighty preoccupations about girls and school evolved through my senior year. I decided, with little debate, to go to Harvard. When my questionnaire arrived from the Selective Service System, I had resolved not to register as a conscientious objector.

It was surprising how little conflict I felt in making the decision once the time had come. The hard part was explaining my choice to my parents, particularly Mother. When I was a child and did something that particularly pleased her, Mother would say in her understated style, "Thee's a very satisfactory little boy." My decisions about Harvard and the draft were the first that ever seriously displeased and disappointed her. My life had clearly entered a new chapter. I was no longer my mother's very satisfactory little boy. I would soon become the possession of the U.S. Army. And, in doing so, I would become my own person.

How did it happen that the decision to enter the armed services was ultimately so easy to make? In a perverse way, my Quaker values were being illuminated by the darkness in Europe. The triumph of monstrous aggression abroad was the central fact of my adolescent years. How could I be a conscientious objector to military service, a position I had learned to understand and revere from a young age, when my own conscience was so clear about the right thing to do? To me it seemed I was becoming a true Quaker, a person of conscience who was joining with the forces of light against the darkness of evil.

I had some secondary and far less noble reasons for

deciding to enter the Army. I wanted to impress my cousins. They were boys I'd grown up with, and I'd always felt a kind of rivalry with them. I excelled in all the categories I cared about—fastest runner, best soccer player, one of the top students in school. But I think I also wanted to prove that I could do something really significant completely on my own. That was a pretty big deal in our large extended family, which was so protective, proud, and beneficently controlling.

Our platoon stayed at Grandmenil for over a week after the front line moved south and east. The Germans had been stopped, but snipers and small pockets of enemy soldiers were fanatically holding on. We were billeted in an old stone farmhouse fronting the dirt road through town and backed by a barnyard and fields. There was new snow almost every night, and the days were cold and damp.

Late one afternoon two tanks from the 7th Armored Division pulled up next to our house, their powerful throaty motors slowly coughing into silence. We found out later they were part of a fast-moving task force sent to help raise the siege of Bastogne, about twenty miles to the south. Their radios were tuned nonstop to the Armed Forces Network, and we listened with delight to the music of Benny Goodman and the news that the Russian Army was driving west toward the German border.

Later that same morning the sky began to fill with huge formations of Flying Fortresses, hundreds upon hundreds everywhere you looked, heading east. In what seemed like only a few seconds, we could see them beginning to drop their bombs. I recall my elation, how we cheered them on. We felt we were seeing the tables turning, the war emphatically going our way. My delight at this incredible sight overwhelmed any possible twinges of Quaker conscience about the horrors taking place at that moment on the ground inside Germany. In fact, I don't think I had any contact with my conscience from the beginning of combat until the war ended. The awfulness of war makes thoughts simple, reactions natural. I learned that only God can judge motives. We were doing what we had to do and thinking what came naturally.

One morning a group of us decided to check out the town's bombed-out church. Why did we even bother to go in? As we stepped over, around, and through the debris, we noticed to our surprise that the organ appeared to be intact. A guy said he'd—what the hell—give it a try. Pushing aside a mess of debris, he began to pump the pedals and hit the keys. And some notes began to come out, notes that sounded like Bach. And it no longer mattered that everything around was broken, that death was only two days behind us. Here we were, a ragged group of men of differing religious backgrounds who were suddenly embraced by the sensation that something like a divinity was right there with us. Soothing and protecting us. Better than a hot shower or a hot meal. Better than a night without guard duty. It was the sound of everlasting life.

I was ill prepared for peace in 1946 when I was discharged at Fort Dix, New Jersey, about twenty-five miles from home. I returned to Harvard that summer, along with a large group of veterans trying to catch up. But it soon became apparent that I had lost both the desire and the ability to catch up with the easy distractions of college life. I couldn't shake, nor did I want to, the recollections of the past three years. I wondered how others could do it.

What was the matter with me? Was it Harvard? Was it the war? For all of us in battle this war had asked for a full measure of wit, nerve, and strength. And mostly luck. Peace made no demands. It was suddenly up to us again to make something worthy of ourselves.

Within seven months I dropped out of Harvard and volunteered for a Quaker work camp back in Europe. Having participated in a war of mass destruction, I had a palpable need to help build things back up. I would later transfer to Haverford, the Quaker college my mother always intended for me, my father's alma mater.

It had taken the experience of war to reawaken the Quaker ideals that had nested in me since childhood. Seeing violence and death firsthand had made the ocean of darkness a vivid reality for me—one that would haunt me for decades to come. I soon learned, however, that repairing the damage of war was a lot more complicated than rebuilding bombed-out villages as a member of a Quaker work camp. All I knew was that I felt more at home in the wrecked shell of Europe than in the ivied walls of Harvard Yard.

I learned some unexpected lessons from being in combat. How alone I was. How much I didn't know about nearly everything. How wrong it was to judge other people, to grade them by our own measure. I also learned that right and wrong are not absolutes— that we must all make our own decisions in matters of conscience. As a child I looked to my community for answers. As an eighteen-year-old Quaker who had never before questioned the fact that my religion provided me with easy answers for just about every problem, I found that this time, I had to make the call myself.

More than half of the draft-eligible Quaker men in the United States served in World War II, inspired by the clear moral choices of this conflict. It was a higher percentage than in any previous war. I believe whole-heartedly that the Quakers who were conscientious objectors did the right thing. They were keeping alive a precious ideal—affirming the role of peacemaker and the place of nonviolence in human affairs. Those who went to war did the right thing too. "Doing the right thing" can only be defined as letting your conscience guide you, as listening to that small voice of God within you, and doing your best to follow the path of truth. The most precious gift life offers us is choice. No one can ever take it away from us. No one but God can ever judge the choices we make.

Shakespeare wrote, in a different context, that "conscience doth make cowards of us all." I think what he meant is that listening to and acting on our conscience is a scary and lonely exercise. We fear our conscience for the same reasons we fear the truth. We know that following our conscience can expose us to ridicule and take away the props that make us feel secure—a group identity, conformity, anonymity. I would argue that letting your life speak through your conscience is liberating in the same way that truth-telling is. It frees you from the judgment of others because you become answerable only to the God that is in you.

We all know right from wrong. It's what defines our humanity. Acting on that knowledge affirms our faith in the idea that *what we do in this life matters*. If we join with others to create an ocean of light, we can banish the forces of darkness. It's not surprising to me that young people are often the most idealistic and the most conscientious among us. Partly it's because they feel as if they have less to lose than older people do. But more importantly, they have not yet been persuaded by cynicism, by the false voice within that says, "It doesn't matter what you do. Your actions, your vote, your words, will never shift the tide against evil. Better to protect what you have and not stick your neck out."

Fifty years after the fact, it's difficult not to take the Allied victory for granted, to view it as inevitable. But it's important to remember how close the ocean of darkness came to enveloping the world in the 1940s— and how crucial it was that the democratic countries, and the individuals who lived there, allied themselves to oppose the evil of fascism. Ironically, the war ended with the frightening specter of a new ocean of darkness: proof for all time of the unimagined destructiveness of nuclear weapons. History teaches us that darkness and death take different forms in every generation, but the challenge of gathering the forces of light and love to oppose them remains the same.

Thankfully, few young people in this generation are likely to be called upon to bear arms for this country. But each of us faces tests of conscience, large and small. Many people don't even know they have a conscience until they give it a voice by letting their lives speak. But once you have located your conscience—whether in youth or in middle age—and once you have heeded its call, you will have found your true self and your true path.

CHAPTER SIX

NONVIOLENCE

A S A BOY, I GOT AN EARLY TASTE of just how challenging living a Quaker life can be. My grandfather's cow produced more milk than our family could
use, so during the Depression he offered the surplus
milk to poor families in the community. Teenage boys
from these families would come by each afternoon to
pick it up. I was much younger and smaller, and they
knew I'd been taught not to hit back, so they took fun
in terrorizing me.

While I accepted nonviolence as the only possible
response to their aggression, it struck me as a highly
impractical strategy. The movies of my childhood fea-
tured heroes who were quick with their fists or their
guns, yet I was always taught that being manly meant
rejecting violence. As those tough kids chased me across
the field shouting threats, I was far from convinced
by the Quaker position on nonviolence. All I knew
was the shame and anger I felt in my heart.

Nonviolence has always been the most paradoxical, counterintuitive, and optimistic of Quaker ideals. Ever since Cain settled his conflict with Abel through premeditated murder, violence and the lust for dominance and revenge have been viewed as inevitable aspects of human relations. The ancient Greeks saw war as a natural state of affairs: "All things come into being and pass through strife," Heraclitus wrote. And throughout time, nations, tribes, and individuals have readily turned to weaponry to exert control or settle differences—while their poets and balladeers celebrated war heroes and the glory of battle.

In the face of this history, the ideals of pacifism, loving forgiveness, and nonviolence seem quixotic at best. And yet Quakers have always referred to their "peace testimony" as the spiritual heart of their belief and practice. For more than three hundred years, they have let their lives speak most clearly, unremittingly, and effectively through their deeds to promote peace.

Where did Friends acquire the grand, even grandiose, notion that we must wage peace throughout the world, that violence must be met by nonviolence and hatred by love? Most cite the words of Jesus, who—in the Sermon on the Mount, one of the most radical and passionate statements ever made—instructed his followers to extend love in place of the sword. "Whosoever smites thee on thy right cheek, turn to him the other also." Jesus' innovative leap of faith in the power of nonviolence has inspired pacifists ever since. George Fox added a Quaker twist to Jesus' words when he exhorted his followers to "take away the occasion of all wars." He reasoned that since each person is endowed with a spark of the divine, violence against any person is violence against God.

But recognizing God in every person is only the beginning. Nonviolence, for Quakers, is by no means a passive or negative concept, a simple thou-shalt-not-kill prohibition. It is, rather, a springboard for action, an ideal that must be transformed into the active pursuit of peace and justice. In the broadest sense, the challenge to Friends is to become the world's peacemakers. This positive, proactive view of nonviolence, I believe, has been one of Quakerism's greatest contributions to society.

In the seventeenth century, the first generation of Quakers suffered the consequences of their pacifism when hundreds were routinely jailed for refusing to serve in the king's militia. In the Revolutionary War, most Quakers refused to bear arms, but an estimated five hundred were "read out" of their Meetings for joining up with the colonial forces. Abraham Lincoln, at the height of the Civil War, wrote to a prominent

Friend, Eliza Gurney, "Your people, the Friends, have had, and are having a very great trial. On principle and faith opposed to both war and oppression, they can only practically oppose oppression by war. In this hard dilemma some have chosen one horn, and some the other."

The American Friends Service Committee, which in 1947 became the first organization to win a Nobel Prize, has been waging peace since World War I through its international relief programs. America's oldest religious lobby, the Friends Committee on National Legislation, has worked continuously for peace and disarmament by supporting the old League of Nations and the United Nations as well as weapons restriction, reduction in the U.S. armed forces, reduction in defense spending, an end to the U.S. bases overseas, and a long list of related issues. Some American Quakers have practiced civil disobedience by mounting public protests against specific American military initiatives. Others have withheld "war taxes"—the percentage of the income tax they believe goes for military purposes. And of course, young Quakers have always wrestled with their consciences, as I did, when confronted with the choice of whether or not to accept conscription into military service.

There are also Quakers who have taken more extreme measures to oppose war. Shortly after the democratic country of Costa Rica disbanded its army in 1948, a group of American Quakers, recognizing an opportunity to support a country that so publicly expressed their religion's most compelling concern, emigrated and became Costa Rican citizens. Tourists visiting the remote northern Monteverde Cloud Forest are often surprised when, on a road traveled by an ox-drawn milk wagon leading to the Quaker cheese factory, they see lines of children, some now third-generation Costa Rican Quakers, walking toward their Friends *Escuela*.

I'll never forget an instance of war protest that drew considerable press attention at the time and evoked responses among Quakers that ran the gamut from intense admiration to utter horror at a violent action of self-destruction. On November 2, 1965, a Quaker named Norman Morrison set himself on fire in front of the Pentagon, outside Secretary of Defense Robert McNamara's office, to protest the Vietnam War. While Buddhism, as practiced in Vietnam, has a tradition of monks immolating themselves to protest injustice, Quakerism has never espoused suicide or violence of any sort.

The tension between the ideal and the necessary will be with us forever. During World War II, I, along with many other Quakers, found myself unable to follow faithfully in the way of the peacemaker because of my concern about the practical consequences for others, who were being so cruelly oppressed. Although I fought in World War II, I have been in full agreement with the pacifist stance of Quakerism in the primarily political and tactical wars this country has entered since that time.

The wish for universal peace has never, of course, been restricted to Quakers. In fact, it is reflected in the liturgy of every world religion. The most revered twentieth-century martyrs to nonviolence were a Hindu and a Baptist: Mahatma Gandhi and Martin Luther King, Jr. The fact that both were loved, honored, and *listened to* by so many people of all faiths is, in itself, a testimony to the yearning of people of this century for an end to violence of all sorts. But even more important than speaking out eloquently for peace, these men became visionary leaders by showing that nonviolence can succeed as a strategy for overcoming the injustice imposed by a more powerful adversary.

Gandhi made *Satyagraha*—civil disobedience based on truth and nonviolence—the basis of his movement to oppose Britain's colonial rule over India. His words and deeds inspired a mass peaceful political protest that spread across the continent, leading to Indian independence in 1948. Following Gandhi's lead, Reverend King used bus boycotts and lunch counter sit-ins to overthrow a century of Jim Crow segregation in America. Both Gandhi and King were deeply spiritual men who understood that nonviolence is not simply an intellectual ideal. It is a commitment of the soul that must be lived every day. Gandhi wrote, "Nonviolence is not a garment to be put on and off at will. Its seat is in the heart, and it must be an inseparable part of our very being."

For Quakers, nonviolence is indeed "an inseparable part of our very being." At its heart, waging peace is an act of love. Shortly after George Fox exhorted his followers to "take away the occasion of all wars," William Penn summed up the philosophy that has guided Quaker peace efforts ever since: "A good end cannot sanctify evil means," he wrote, "nor must we ever do evil, that good may come of it. . . . Let us then try what love will do."

"Trying what love will do" involves, first, looking inward. Guided by the divine light, we can discover the best that is in us, which is truth and love. We must then look outward for ways to put the power of our love to work in the world. Quakers have always viewed social injustice as the root of all violence, and the desire to right injustice is the starting point of "trying what love can do." When Quakers first came to the New World, they found the earlier settlers exploiting the native population. Friends treated the Indians fairly, paying fair prices for land they owned and starting schools for their children. As a result, many Quakers lived unharmed in the midst of what was considered hostile Indian territory. Most Quakers were strongly opposed to slavery, and many were avid abolitionists who helped bring slaves north through the Underground Railroad. Wherever they've encountered the oppressed and disenfranchised—the poor, the imprisoned, and the mentally ill—Quakers have tried to put love to work.

Even when this meant extending love to the enemy. The American Friends Service Committee has always carried out its relief work without regard to whether recipients were perceived as political allies. After World War I, the AFSC saved thousands of German civilians from starvation. The goodwill that accrued from these feeding programs allowed Quakers to travel to Germany in 1938 and arrange exit routes for an untold number of Jews who would surely have died in concentration camps.

"Trying what love can do" to effect international peace and end violence on the home front can seem a far more elusive goal today than it was for early Quakers. The tensions and complexities of modern life, dramatically escalated and writ large by global politics, make peacemaking incredibly difficult, for many a hopeless goal, little more than a staple of political rhetoric.

Yet Quakerism, with its belief in the perfectibility of human nature, is relentlessly optimistic. For most people, cynicism intrudes on belief in the power of nonviolence. A leap of faith is required if we are to believe that nonviolence can heal a violent world, that turning the other cheek when struck, instead of striking back, can end a fight. We need faith to believe that by loving our enemy we can eventually transform him into an ally; that even when nonviolence fails to achieve peace, it can succeed in curing hate.

In 1936, as Europe massed for yet another terrible conflict, Carl Sandburg gave voice to the dream of peace when he wrote, "Sometime they'll give a war and nobody will come." If we share that wish today, then each of us must find a way to wage peace.

But where do we begin?

Since most of us won't be called upon to take up arms for our country or to become peace emissaries overseas, the most obvious place to begin confronting violence is in our own lives. The majority of us are not brawlers, wife-beaters, or murderers. We are not uncontrollably driven by brutal instincts and are shocked and alarmed by others who are. Yet each of us is capable of hostile thoughts and hostile acts. We know what it means to "kill with a look" or wound someone's feelings with intent. We all wield emotional or economic power over others, and all too often we betray that trust.

Whether we begin to mend the world in our own backyard or on the other side of the globe, love is the only tool we need. In 1937, a year after Carl Sandburg wished for a no-show war, a world gathering of Quakers convened in London and issued this statement: "For all the tasks before us—whether of the family, the social order, witnessing for peace or for a true way of living, the responsibility is a personal one. We must learn to walk in that way which is truth and which alone leads to life—the way of persuading, self-giving, compassionate love."

Nonviolence—which always flows from love—is indisputably a practical ideal because it leads to beneficial results: a warmer social climate, a more humane community, a less vicious world. Of course, most Quakers would cite the added personal benefit of pursuing nonviolence: peace of mind and heart. Hate poisons the soul; love and forgiveness enrich it. If we hope to overcome the ocean of darkness in the world, we must first light a candle in our own hearts. And as Jesus discovered on the Mount—and as people of all religions have since discovered—committing oneself to the path of love can be the most revolutionary way to change the world.

For parents, changing the world often translates into raising a more humane generation of young people. But teaching our children to reject violence is a daunting responsibility. How do we teach gentleness and love to boys and girls who are exposed from their earliest years to the sort of raw and senseless violence that pervades the media? What are children to make of television's wanton display of cruelty, shooting, stabbing, explosions? We can support program rating and supervise our children's exposure, but we know this is only feasible in their earliest years.

Many gentle and well-meaning parents are pained to recognize that almost every boy falls in love with weaponry at a young age. Any boy at play will take a stick and turn it into a gun. I'm afraid I'll have to leave it to the psychiatrists to explain why kids are so strongly attracted to guns and gore, but the toy industry has certainly responded. The squirt guns and plastic swords of my children's early years have given way to a proliferation of armaments that boggle the imagination— many of them aggressively promoted on children's television programs. Whether by nature or nurture, children are attracted to these products. As parents, we need to face this fact, not deny it or shrug it off as biological destiny. It's within our power to educate young people about the cause-and-effect reality of guns, the truth of the Turkish proverb, "A weapon is an enemy even to its owner."

A visit to Toys "R" Us with my grandson Ben, then aged six, was an alarming eye-opener to this out-of-touch grandfather. Our mission was to buy a checker set. I had sentimental visions of reenacting the many hours I spent playing checkers and later chess with my own grandfather, and I was eager to introduce Ben to the game. I was directed to the correct section of this big, bewildering store, and was momentarily re-assured to find that checker sets were still being sold. But our route to the board-games shelves took us down an aisle stacked with hundreds of brawny action figures, all toting guns. I don't think I need mention that they looked a whole lot more exciting to Ben than the checker set.

Soon afterward my son, Geoff, and his wife, Sarah, were startled when, on a visit to the Lake Champlain Maritime Museum in New York State, they found that Ben was entranced, to the exclusion of all other displays, by the cannons on a model gunship. Soon after the museum visit Ben was given an illustrated Bible designed for children and became transfixed by the pictures of the Stations of the Cross. "I like this book," he said enthusiastically to his dismayed parents, "because of all the bloody stuff in it."

How can we counter children's attraction to violence? My response is that family intimacy is the only antidote you can rely on. Certainly, the techniques of nonviolent conflict resolution, now taught widely in management programs and increasingly in schools, are catching on in the most gratifying way. My grandson Christopher, now a fourth-grader, is studying the subject. At recess he and classmates don hats labeled Trouble Tromper. When two or more kids get into an argument, or if someone is simply being obnoxious, along come the Trouble Trompers. "We go over and see if they want a mediator," he tells me with delight, "and we get them to settle things themselves or we brainstorm solutions. We try to get down to the real reason for the situation, not just the top layer." Christopher takes great pride in his identity as a peacemaker.

According to a woman who teaches techniques of nonviolence, quite young children respond enthusiastically to ideas such as active listening and avoiding judgmental language. They have a deep-seated need, she says, to do the right thing. Peer mediation programs in high schools have been enormously successful, and workshops on prejudice reduction and diversity round-tables in workplaces and schools are routinely over-subscribed.

But paying lip service to peace—and even teaching it in school—isn't enough. If we truly hope to mold young hearts and minds to the ideal of nonviolence, we need to teach it by example at home. Children observe the ways their parents treat each other and the people in their employ. And children have an acute under-standing of how powerless they are in a world of adults. They look to us for love and encouragement and fair-ness. Building a close and loving home where each in-dividual feels respected and loved is the only true antidote to the influence of a violent society and violence-crazed media. Only in the atmosphere of a close and loving home can parents transmit values based on love and forgiveness.

I have always recognized the influence that schools—where children spend more time per day than with their families—can have on children's moral de-velopment. I was particularly concerned about this issue in the 1960s, when I was headmaster of the country's largest Quaker day school, Sidwell Friends. Two de-cades after fighting in World War II, I had to decide how active a role our school would play in opposing the Vietnam War. On one hand, I identified with our fighting men on the ground and always opposed their vilification by the upper-middle-class men at the center of the antiwar movement who were at little personal risk of being drafted. But it was clear to me and to all of us in the Quaker community that this was an armed conflict we needed to oppose, even in its early stages when the country had not yet awakened to the immorality of the war.

Most of all, I felt it was important for the high-school students—after examining their own consciences—to make a personal choice about how to respond to their government's foreign policy. That they attended a Quaker school or had a teacher who was an ardent antiwar activist should not, I felt, determine their viewpoint. The soul-searching I underwent when our nation went to war and I was seventeen led me to the horrors of the battlefront, but it reinforced a lifetime habit of trying to live truthfully.

Vietnam is already a generation past, but in every decade we are confronted with personal choices about whether to support or oppose our country's military operations around the world, from Grenada to the Persian Gulf, from Somalia to Bosnia. As citizens of the last military superpower and de facto world policemen, all Americans carry a special responsibility to let our lives speak as a force for peace.

The paradox remains as perplexing today as ever: How can we effectively oppose violence without descending into violence?

The genius of nonviolence lies in its marriage of idealism and pragmatism. In a recent bow to pragmatism, which I personally applaud, several Friends Meetings have decided to support the use of "peacekeeping forces" (a term that used to sound contradictory to me) in the former Yugoslavia. And for all the criticism heaped on the United Nations, it supports a remarkable array of economic peacebuilding efforts around the world that benefit millions of people.

Two thousand years ago, Jesus preached that justice founded on the principle of "an eye for an eye" would eventually create a world of blind men. Today, living in the nuclear age, we have no practical alternative to pursuing peace. As Martin Luther King, Jr., said, "At the center of nonviolence stands the principle of life. . . . It is no longer a choice between violence and nonviolence in this world, it's nonviolence or nonexistence."

The fact is, each of us can become a peacekeeper in a small corner of our world—whether at home or in our community. All we need to bring to the task is love, and the will to bestow it more generously than we have in the past. Poets and philosophers have constructed an elaborate calculus of love. Quakers ask that we only do simple addition. The more love we add to the world, the more loving and humane a place it will become. We each have a lot more impact on the world and people around us than we realize, and in particular on the young people in our lives. Acknowledging this fact, and the awesome responsibility it carries, is as good a starting point as any for our ongoing journey toward peace.

CHAPTER SEVEN

SERVICE

HERE'S A QUAKER JOKE. A Friend takes a non-Quaker to Meeting for Worship. Everyone is sitting quietly with heads down and eyes closed. After five or ten minutes of continued silence the visitor becomes increasingly restless and puzzled. He nudges the Quaker and asks in a loud whisper, "When does the service begin?" The Quaker replies, "The service begins when the worship ends."

Not exactly a knee-slapper, but then Quakers have never distinguished themselves as humorists. The point of the story is that for Quakers there is a direct link between worship and service to others. The search for truth, which begins in contemplation, finds expression in action. Despite the inward direction of Quaker worship, Friends are by nature activist, not monastic. They believe that the reason we were put on earth is to help each other, to make this a better world. William Penn linked worship and service succinctly when he said,

"True Godliness does not turn men out of the world but enables them to live better in it, and excites their endeavors to mend it."

The concept of Quaker service starts with the belief that there is that of God in every person and that all people in the world are, therefore, members of one extended family of equals. What can we do to make this miraculous family of ours healthier, happier, less violent? The first generations of Quakers in this country took up the challenge by working for the abolition of slavery, fair treatment of Indians, and humane conditions for prisoners and patients in mental hospitals. Two hundred and fifty years later, the Nobel Prize for Peace was awarded to the American Friends Service Committee with this eloquent citation: "It is the silent help from the nameless to the nameless which is their contribution to the promotion of brotherhood among nations." True service, Quakers believe, responds to need wherever it exists in the human family—not simply to the problems of our direct kin, close friends, and political allies.

A recent biography of the late civil-rights leader Bayard Rustin, a Quaker who studied and taught techniques of Gandhian nonviolence, quotes Rustin as saying: "My activism did not spring from being black. Rather, it is rooted fundamentally in my Quaker upbringing and the values instilled in me by the grand-parents who reared me. Those values were based on the concept of a single human family and the belief that all members of that family are equal."

Although only Quakers speak of the divine spark that unites the human family, all religions encourage their followers to "love thy neighbor as thyself," to care for the stranger, the widow, and the orphan. They may quote different authorities in support of their views— the Gospels, the Talmud, the Koran, or the Book of Mormon—but the end message is the same. The story of the Good Samaritan is as relevant today as in biblical times; it's the small acts of human kindness to needy strangers that best express our humanity.

Consider this commonplace urban dilemma. On your route to work, two or three panhandlers have staked out street corners that you must pass every morning. They are ragged and unwashed; you are clean-shaven and well pressed. They have nothing; you have a home, a family, a job. And yet they have the power to make you cross the street and go blocks out of your way to avoid encountering them.

It's not that parting with a few coins is so painful. En route to work, we may already have spent five dol-lars on coffee, newspapers, and bus or subway fare. What feels so costly is facing the disparity between ourselves and another human being. Even if we pass by without acknowledging the outstretched hand and the mumbled request for spare change, we can't escape such a flagrant display of life's unfairness. Why is this person sick, addicted to drugs, homeless, while I have a job, a home, good health, and a family?

I make a conscious effort to resist the urge to ignore street people. And I try to recognize the needy person's humanity by extending a smile and a kind word along with a few coins. I don't do this only because it makes me feel less guilty—which it does. When we walk past an indigent person without even a nod of recognition, we deny the existence of God in that person. When we pretend that he or she is invisible, we blind ourselves to that person's inner light and its connection to our own.

Altruism presents the same paradox as nonviolence. Like turning the other cheek, helping the stranger is a fundamentally counterintuitive act. We humans, like all other creatures, are basically a self-interested species. Our instinct is to husband our resources and share them only with close family and friends—people we know well and love and who are likely to reciprocate when we ourselves are in need. Why, after all, should we care about strangers?

My belief is that altruism is actually a deep-seated

human instinct, that we all have a mysterious drive to express the best that is in us. When we listen for and hear the cries of the needy, the oppressed, or the sick, something inside us instinctively responds. The evidence of this altruistic instinct can be found in the fact that one in three Americans engages in voluntary community service, and collectively we donate billions of dollars a year to charitable organizations.

But we are also driven by a countervailing instinct: our fear of the unknown, of people whose cultures and values we don't understand. This tug-of-war between our fear of strangers and our need to connect with those outside our own experience is the dynamic force that draws men and women to each other, and drives them apart. It's what moves us to travel to foreign lands and meet foreign people, and what compels us to erect Berlin Walls and adopt restrictive immigration policies. Service to others is the way we break down the walls that keep us isolated in our own lives and in our own communities. It's how we grow as human beings.

My first experience with helping strangers was an eye-opener, a maturing event that no one had prepared me for. I had grown up in astonishingly sheltered circumstances in Moorestown, New Jersey, then a majority-Quaker town. I lived there surrounded by gentle and fond relatives, schoolmasters, and friends. All the people I knew looked alike and, except at election time, thought alike, too. Our home was simple but comfortable, our lifestyle necessarily more frugal than that of many of our relatives. But although I read regularly in the *Philadelphia Record* about the millions of people left destitute by the Depression, I had no direct exposure to poverty.

One day when I was fourteen, all that changed. My history teacher, David Richie, a young activist Quaker and something of a Pied Piper, invited the class to participate in a weekend work camp he had begun in a run-down section of northeast Philadelphia. I found myself, a mere twenty miles from home, in an impoverished, violence-ridden, black ghetto. The people I was working with seemed, at first, totally different from anyone I knew. Each weekend I helped "my family" paint their house and make repairs, and together we admired the results of our efforts.

Those weekends provided my first recognition that you learn about life through interactions with others who are different from yourself, not by looking inward. Doing physical labor side by side with total strangers who needed help taught me lessons that went far beyond anything I had learned in a classroom or in Meeting about the commonality that transcends differences, about the kinship engendered by shared labor. I benefited as much by my efforts as the family I was trying to help. I learned that not only are we our brother's keepers, our brother is *our* keeper too—the keeper of our soul.

Mr. Richie, who drew no distinction between "service" and "work," offered his students a simple definition of service that has stayed with me ever since. "Work," he said, "is love made visible."

This truth came home to me in a different context ten years later. After returning from the war, I had enormous difficulty reentering college life. The concerns of my classmates at Harvard seemed trivial and the confines of the classroom walls almost suffocating. I left school and returned to Belgium and France sixteen months after I departed as a soldier, eager to begin rebuilding countries I had so recently helped destroy.

My first assignment was in the western Belgian mining community of Bossus Bois. I was there to help an international team of students build a community soccer field in an area covered by ugly slag heaps from the nearby abandoned coal mines. Two years after pushing machine-gun and rifle ammunition through the Ardennes forest, I now found myself only thirty miles way, digging slag and hauling it away in iron carts from dawn till dusk. It was the hardest physical labor I'd ever done—and I'd never been so happy. It didn't feel like penance or like charity. I was giving something tangible to people in need—a playing field for children recovering from a war—and it was making *me* feel whole. This work absolutely seemed like "love made visible" and yet, *I* was the one who felt loved. I realized that, like nonviolence, service blends idealism and pragmatism. Giving of ourselves to help others works in two ways: It benefits the recipient and it benefits the giver.

I learned a tougher truth about service while working in the Mexican village of Yautepec during a summer off from Haverford College, where I'd transferred from Harvard. I had joined an AFSC work camp with other Quaker college and high-school students to dig privies and convey to families in our crude Spanish the importance of good sanitation. We were trying to lessen the incidence of dysentery, but the local people viewed us with hostility and suspicion. The priest, dead set against us, told people we were in town to stir up trouble and proselytize.

As difficult as my Mexican experience was, it taught me the most important lesson about service. The point is to keep working at a job you believe is valuable and hope it makes life better for others, whether or not you see immediate improvement. Service has the potential for intense gratification and also for big-time disappointment. The sense of fulfillment in all altruistic efforts must come from the doing, not from tangible results—and certainly not from expressions of gratitude from the people you're trying to help. The Indian poet Rabindranath Tagore expressed this idea in a few lines when he wrote:

"Let me light my lamp,"
 Says the star,
"And never debate
 If it will help to remove the darkness."

Volunteer work in a good cause can become a lifetime commitment. And since career choices are most often made in youth, it's of critical importance that young people have a direct experience of service and all its enriching possibilities. A "good job" used to be defined as one that paid more than a "not-so-good job," but more and more young men and women are now entering careers that offer not simply a living but an opportunity to make a difference in the world. They want a career that reflects both their interests and their ideals, and the range of opportunities is enormous. Reading the alumni notes from Sidwell Friends School, I'm amazed at the multitude of service-related careers former students are pursuing that my Quaker forebears never imagined: advising banks on loans to low-income people, working on wetlands preservation, making educational films for children's television. The list includes work in nonprofit and for-profit institutions—even in business.

People of my generation defined the service or "helping" professions pretty narrowly. The list was headed by medicine, education, and social work, all fields in which Quakers are very well represented. My mother, unlike her brothers, was not encouraged to seek a career in medicine—so few women were in those days. She gravitated naturally to social work and found intense gratification in the one-on-one case work she did before marriage. When Molly and Nancy and I were teenagers, she reentered the workforce, helping the rural poor near Riverton, New Jersey. She brought to her job considerable expertise about the social and medical services available to these very needy, often quite isolated people. But she also brought love, love that was never spoken but that was made visible in ways that said far more than words.

She was even able to get through to a notoriously grouchy hermit named Eval Chambers, a needy and sick man staunchly resistant to being helped. I had once glimpsed him in his orchard, a dark figure with his head turned away. In my imagination, Chambers was a scary guy with a scary name who lived alone up in the hills.

I always heard his first name as "Evil," although I knew it really wasn't spelled that way. But somehow Mother succeeded where others had failed. Thoreau once wrote, in a particularly reclusive mood, "If I knew for a certainty that a man was coming to my house with the conscious design of doing me good, I should run for my life." That was a good description of Chambers, the man who turned away all efforts of assistance until Mother took on his case and, through extending love, was able to help him.

I decided early in my teenage years that medicine would probably be my profession, a decision that was based on admiration for my grandfathers and uncles rather than on my academic strengths. One of my most vivid early memories is of my Uncle Joe, a well-known pediatrician and head of Philadelphia Children's Hospital, setting forth in the middle of a huge, festive Christmas dinner at Aunt Sally's in Germantown to visit a sick child. We saw Great-aunt Sally and the full array of cousins, uncles, and aunts only at the holiday dinners she held for the entire family, and it would ordinarily have been unthinkable to miss a minute of the merry goings-on. But I was eager to accompany Uncle Joe, so he took me along. We traveled through the dreary North Philadelphia slums on our way to the home of a young boy of about my age who had contracted polio during the previous summer.

The apartment was drab and unadorned, even on Christmas Day. Because of fear of contagion, I was told to wait in the kitchen, but peering down the hall I could make out the scene in the far bedroom. Uncle Joe pulled up a chair and examined the boy, gently unbuttoning his pajama shirt and probing his chest with a stethoscope. Meanwhile, his parents hovered anxiously at the foot of the bed, holding hands. When he was done with his examination, Uncle Joe engaged the parents in some light conversation that managed to draw a laugh from everyone in that cramped little room.

It seemed to me the truest expression of the spirit of Christmas. My uncle, one of the pioneers in early efforts to develop a polio vaccine, was bringing comfort to a family of strangers on Christmas Day. He was trying, by every means known, to save a boy he had never seen before and give hope to his family. I was in awe of the extraordinary power that resided in this one skillful and compassionate man.

When we returned to the car Uncle Joe was deep in thought, but finally he spoke to me, saying he thought the boy had "a good chance." I decided then and there that I would also be a doctor, because I wanted to make my life as useful as his. I had no shortage of physician role models in the family. The Smiths—my father's father and grandfather—were doctors in inner-city Philadelphia. My mother's father, Grandfather Stokes, decided on the life of a small-town doctor when he was a boy, seeing himself as a link in an unbroken chain of dedicated healers.

The first Stokes doctor, John Hinchman Stokes, opened his practice in Moorestown in 1785, and his descendants worked in our town as family practitioners generation after generation. In Grandfather's family history he wrote of the life of John Hinchman Stokes, who was born in 1764 into a family of farmers but was sent to learn medicine because he was considered too physically delicate for farming. He became an enlightened physician who was so impressed with Dr. Jenner's new smallpox vaccine that he vaccinated his small daughter and laid her in bed with one of his patients to convince the skeptics that the wondrous new discovery really worked.

Reading about this pioneer, I understood why his sons and grandsons, who formed an unbroken chain as family practitioners in our small town, were inspired to follow in his footsteps. And, although small-town general practice was by no means the exclusive province of Friends, I felt that these Quaker doctors brought to their work an added dimension, which I would call faith. Faith that the power of intellect and caring could make a sick person well; faith that the human condition was perfectible, and that the power of science, lovingly administered, could help spread light into lives darkened by illness. My Grandfather Stokes's Quaker faith—rooted in the search for truth, belief in the equality of all people, and a commitment to service—shaped both his public and private conduct. As I remember him and his healing role in the community, where he also served on numerous boards and committees, I recognize in him qualities that are far from commonplace in today's medical environment—a buoyant and loving optimism, a drive toward perfection, a readiness to speak to the best in every person.

The compelling urge to heal, to make ourselves and others whole, is what might be called a Quaker obsession. Quakers trace their healing instinct to George Fox, whose earliest revelations healed him from unbearable inner suffering, and whose famous *Journal* is a day-by-day account of his efforts to heal others. But the fact that so many Quakers became doctors can also be traced to discrimination. In the early years, Quakers were barred from attending Oxford or Cambridge because they were not members of the Church of England. The only profession they could study in Edinburgh, where the university *did* accept Quakers, was medicine. Later, in America, when Quakers started their own schools, colleges, and universities, science was always a strong subject. Unlike some sects, Quakerism has never viewed science as a threat to religion. On the contrary, Quakers have always embraced scientific inquiry as a search after truth concerning God's creation.

In this spirit, Quakers established the first humane institutions for the mentally ill in this country. At a time when insanity was considered evidence of moral decay, Friends honored the divine spark that they recognized in even the most deeply disturbed human beings. The earliest facility that treated victims of mental disease as sick people rather than criminals or clowns was founded in 1669 by English Quaker William Tuck, who also became the first doctor to attempt treating these patients without the use of mechanical restraints. In all other institutions the mentally ill were cruelly restrained, beaten, and often exhibited for the amusement of the villagers. In the mid-eighteenth century, Quakers established the Friends Hospital near Philadelphia, guided by the desire to cure rather than punish the afflicted. During World War II a large number of Quaker conscientious objectors followed in this tradition and served very effectively as ward attendants in mental hospitals.

Grandfather Stokes and his two doctor sons, Uncle Joe and Uncle Emlen, took pride in the history of Friends' treatment of the mentally ill. Which is why I was surprised that, although they applauded my early interest in going into medicine, all three disparaged my intention of becoming a psychiatrist. I had never actually met anyone in this exotic field, but it seemed to me to offer opportunities to make people's lives better in a particularly intense person-to-person manner. We were all pretty straitlaced in my family, and it may be that they were shocked by Freud's revolutionary views on childhood sexuality—so shocked that they could never discuss the subject, at least not in my presence. What did come across to me clearly was that these hands-on healers had, like most of their colleagues, more than a little skepticism about a "talking cure" whose therapeutic power was difficult to measure by scientific methods.

In my own lifetime, the medical search after truth has resulted in extraordinary progress in relieving human suffering, curing disease, and increasing longevity. Doctors have much more effective therapies to offer patients than they did when I was a child, and polio and other dread diseases have been virtually eradicated worldwide. But I share the dismay most Americans feel about the increasingly impersonal, bottom-line approach to medicine in this country and the uneven distribution of health care. It would be hard for Grandfather, who died in 1947, to believe that despite great advances in preventive medicine, an estimated 40 million Americans still have little or no medical insurance, that in this richest nation on earth children go without inoculations and women do without prenatal care. Since Grandfather's commitment to healing was rooted in the belief that there is that of God in every person, he never questioned that all people had a God-given right to the same quality and quantity of medical attention. In his practice, illness or injury were the only qualifications any man, woman, or child needed to receive the best medical treatment he could render.

He would, however, be pleased to see that family practitioners, or "primary care physicians" as they're now called, are making a comeback. Each year, for twenty years, Grandfather was invited by the dean of his alma mater, the University of Pennsylvania Medical School, to address the graduating class. And each year he decried the increasingly popular choice of specialization and urged that young doctors consider family practice. As early as the 1930s he drew the students' attention to the waning number of physicians in rural areas, an issue that is now more urgent than ever.

Grandfather ended his speech by distinguishing between pleasure and happiness. To him pleasure was something that could be bought—entertainment, trips to Europe, and other diversions that he considered nonessentials. Happiness was what primarily interested him, and in his view a happy life was the virtually inevitable result of being a small-town family doctor, seeing the same patients and their families year after year, coming to understand their lives, not simply their illnesses. He carried in his pocket a copy of these lines spoken by the young country doctor in George Eliot's *Middlemarch*: "I could never have been happy in any profession which did not involve the highest intellectual strain and yet kept me in good warm contact with my neighbors."

When I left for college, my grandfather, anticipating that I would be the next doctor in the family, gave me the beautiful old microscope he had used in medical school. But my plans for a medical career crashed during my first year at Harvard. I took two lab sciences, biology and chemistry, and just escaped failing both, although I had no problems at all with my classes in English and philosophy and history. By sophomore year

I had faced up to my shameful lack of ability in science and eliminated medical school as a goal. It seemed to me at the time that the door to the fullest life I could give myself had slammed shut.

"As way opens" is a Quaker saying that stems directly from Meeting, from the experience of patiently seeking truth through group silence. It also pertains more broadly to discovering your own capabilities and your own individual path. And so it happened with me. I became a philosophy major and, later, a graduate student in English at Columbia and an instructor in its School of General Studies. I recognized with high enthusiasm that in my search for a service-oriented career, the way had opened for me in the field of education. I still have Grandfather's microscope, and when I look at it, it reminds me not of failure but of success in finding my own talent, my own useful place in a profession that offered, each day and in myriad ways, significant opportunities for service.

What is the importance of service, of trying to help people you don't know or of struggling in a cause that may not reach fruition in your lifetime? Former congresswoman Shirley Chisholm suggested, "Service is the rent you pay for having a room on the earth." Woodrow Wilson gave voice to the same sentiment eighty years ago: "There is something better, if possible, that a man can give than his life—that is his living spirit to a service that is not easy."

The simple insight that "work is love made visible" tells us a great deal about letting our lives speak. In the final tally, love is the most instinctive and powerful force in our lives, a gift we should all be more profligate in bestowing on others. I believe that we are most ourselves when we are connecting with others through service. The impulse to serve is the mysterious ingredient that fills us up, that makes our cup run over.

It really doesn't matter where or how we start. It is only important to begin. In the nineteenth century, Lucretia Mott, the tiny, fearless Quaker from Nantucket, made her life speak by working tirelessly for the abolition of slavery, for equal rights, and for higher education for women. Encouraging less active Quakers to become involved in service, she threw out this challenge: "The Light is available yesterday, today and to eternity. What is thee doing about it?"

CHAPTER EIGHT

BUSINESS

ALTHOUGH WE DON'T ORDINARILY think of business as a service profession, many Quakers have let their lives speak by building businesses that truly serve their communities. These independent entrepreneurs saw no conflict between an interest in trade and the call to service.

Commerce is an inseparable part of our daily lives. We depend on merchants to supply us with goods and services, and they depend on our patronage. This country, more than most, is built on the premise of progress through industrial expansion. "The chief business of the American people is business," declared President Calvin Coolidge, giving this sentiment the ring of a national motto.

Yet we Americans have always had a love/hate relationship with big business and high finance. Entrepreneur millionaires of the past and present are canonized in our cultural mythology, but we also see many of them as cutthroat capitalists who made their fortunes through exploitation and deceit. Journalists lavish the breathless prose once reserved for film stars or athletes on profiles of today's stars of the business world, particularly those who are young or photogenic. But after we read them we let out a cynical sigh. What sort of business practices enabled those people to best their competitors and come out on top? Are the products they're selling destructive to health, dangerous for children, overpriced, misadvertised?

This deep-seated distrust extends to our consumer culture. In earlier years proprietors who offered quality merchandise at fair prices gained a reputation for reliability, and their customers rewarded them with loyalty. We look back wistfully at the small shoe stores, independent drugstores, local haberdasheries, whose owners and salespeople were highly regarded in the community. The same men and women served you year after year, and when you asked questions about the quality of an item you were about to buy, you knew you could trust the answer. Today, we only see them in the movies. Old movies.

I noticed recently that, in an effort to gain back our loyalty and trust, certain car dealerships are now making "no-negotiation pricing" a centerpiece of their advertising campaigns. This purportedly new discovery—

that customers like having a set price tag, particularly on high-ticket items—would have amused my Quaker ancestors. Three hundred years ago, in an era when bargaining was the rule, Quakers broke new ground by establishing the one-price system. After determining the proper charge for an item, storekeepers set a fixed price, unlike other merchants who asked more than they expected to get and then engaged in negotiations with the buyer. People could send a child to make a purchase at a Quaker store because they knew the price would always be the same and treatment of the customer would be fair. And although Quaker businesspeople never spoke of or appeared to aim for high profits, the Quaker way of doing business led, almost inevitably, to success.

Friends who made their living in business always considered themselves Quakers first and businesspeople second. Yet I believe that the model of business practice they adhered to, whether they were small tradesmen or major industrialists, offers a simple but profound example for anyone who hopes to run an ethical and profitable business today. Friends organized their workplaces as an expression of the way they conducted their lives, treating all people as equals—employees, customers, business associates—and adhering strictly to the truth in all transactions. Generations of these businesspeople prospered without compromising the best interests of their staff or their customers, letting their lives speak by making the supply of goods a true service to the community.

For Quakers in colonial days, going into business was often less a choice than a process of elimination. Although they enjoyed very high literacy rates for the period, seventeenth-century Friends were excluded from most universities and from positions in public office. Their testimony against war kept them out of the military and politics. Establishing a small business became a popular option for people devoted to independence, hard work, and thrift.

Because Friends always shunned luxury and frivolous spending, the small businessmen of early years focused on providing a limited range of necessities. They were tailors, hatters, printers, booksellers, undertakers. Since trading by ship involved using guns for the protection of goods, they rarely became exporters or importers. Quaker ironmongers refused to make weapons and manufactured much-needed cookware instead. Clothing made by Quaker tailors lacked the laces and ruffles most people favored. And because some dyes were the product of slave labor, many Quakers refused to wear or make clothing of colored cloth.

Despite these limitations, most of these small busi-

nesses prospered. And when they did, Quaker tradesmen began to worry about letting an interest in
commerce dominate their lives. Early merchants often
wrote of reducing or refusing to expand booming businesses because their enterprises were taking too much
time from their spiritual and communal responsibilities.
John Woolman, the saintly Quaker abolitionist, was a
successful tailor, merchant, and grafter of fruit trees who
suffered great anxiety about his worldly success. As he
wrote in his *Journal*, "The increase of business became
my burden." He struggled with the problem for some
time and finally put the question to God, who "gave
me a heart resigned to His Holy will; I then lessened
my outward business."

Because Quaker businessmen enjoyed such a high
reputation for honesty and for offering goods of high
quality, the Quaker Oats Company, which was *not*
started by Quakers, hit on the idea of using the name
as a trademark for their cereal products. The original
picture on the Quaker Oats box showed a drab little
man in early-nineteenth-century Quaker garb who, as
the years passed, evolved into the beaming, ruddy fellow we see today—a beefy guy in a huge hat who looks
a bit like a cross between Benjamin Franklin and Santa
Claus, and who seems about to leap from the box and
give the oats-eater a bear hug. Frankly, not all Quakers

are charmed by this internationally recognized, aggressively ebullient pitchman.

The congenial and optimistic Quaker businessmen in my extended family were a much more restrained lot. They were practical and conservative men, actively involved on numerous Quaker and civic boards and committees and characterized by a typical Quaker plainness of appearance and lifestyle. Most were conspicuously nonmaterialistic. A memorable exception was Uncle Whitall, who owned a beautiful green Pierce-Arrow touring car, an exotic automobile that symbolized his success as an executive at the Whitall-Tatum Glass Company. He often twitted Grandfather, his more serious brother-in-law, for purchasing one "sensible" Buick after another.

All these men were staunch Republicans who adored the Quaker president Herbert Hoover, the first president I can remember. Hoover, a highly successful businessman who had also led the program to feed starving Germans after World War I, was a plain-faced, familiarly dowdy-looking Friend who, as president, advocated sensible-sounding, nonradical approaches to combatting the Great Depression. My uncles and cousins thought he could do no wrong. (My father, who met with more modest business success as a life insurance salesman, was an equally staunch Democrat who thought Hoover could do no right—a shocking stance in our cohesive Quaker family.)

Although these businessmen were, by most standards, prosperous, money was as taboo a subject of discussion as sex in our family. If anyone I knew had a dream of acquiring riches and living a life of luxury, they sure didn't talk about it. The Quaker view was that people who had incomes that far outstripped their needs should consider their wealth a means of doing good works. Philanthropic Quaker businesspeople used their profits to establish and support schools, colleges, hospitals, and other institutions that worked for the benefit of Quakers and non-Quakers in this country and around the world. They also offered employees long time-off periods to serve with the American Friends Service Committee or other Quaker-sponsored volunteer programs.

Despite their conservative ways, Quakers have always been noted for their willingness to innovate, to experiment with doing things in a more efficient way. I think this openness, which has served them well in the world of business, stems from Friends' optimistic view of the perfectibility of human beings and their institutions and even more directly from Quaker Meeting for Worship and its concept of continuing revelation. Friends believe that if they open their hearts and minds, they will receive new truths through the divine light within. Quaker Meetings for Business are driven by the same principle. If a difficult decision must be made, Friends often precede their discussion with an interim of silence, a period in which all wait for truth to emerge "as way opens." I believe that this habit of patiently searching for the way of truth carried over into Friends' eagerness to explore new ways of conducting business and manufacturing a product.

Cousin Fran Stokes, who lived up the street and dropped in often to tell us jokes and stories, ran the Stokes Tomato Company, where he developed the seeds for the tomatoes sold to Campbell's Soups, located down the road in Camden. A typical Quaker entrepreneur, he was a pioneer in the hybridization of tomato plants and also in the vitamin enrichment of juice. One year he concocted a product he named Gusto, a precursor of V8 juice, and ran taste tests in his living room. Mother and Dad and Molly and Nancy and I sat in a circle, earnestly sipping from little paper cups filled with the new drink, and we gave it our official stamp of approval. Just the name was thrilling enough for me! After World War II Cousin Fran arranged, through an organization called Russian War Relief, to send the Soviet Union large quantities of seeds to help reestablish their war-ravaged farming capacities and meet their terrible food shortages.

The well-known Quaker virtue of frugality has also served to bring heightened efficiency to their businesses and industries. Waste is anathema to Friends, and many have shown remarkable ingenuity in finding new ways to eliminate it. When Cousin Fran began raising excessively large crops of celery, an ingredient in Gusto, he decided to start a manufacturing plant to can celery juice. (Although the new product was indisputably nutritious, it wasn't much of a success.) Ever inventive, he developed a method for purifying stream and river water that had been used to wash coal. Other Quaker industrialists sought methods of conserving such precious resources as water and electricity long before environmentalists alerted all of us to this challenge.

Quakers have always recognized that the most valuable and nonrenewable resource of any healthy business is the people who work in it, and their labor practices have reflected that belief. After the industrial revolution, Friends moved far beyond shopkeeping. They established iron and steel foundries, glassworks, chemical plants. They became owners of insurance companies, large banks, and hotels. Despite the growth of their operations, they set a high standard for

employer-employee relations, always based on the concept of the equality of all people.

In England, three Quaker families—Cadbury, Fry,
and Rowntree—established major cocoa and chocolate
manufacturing firms and later built model communities
where their employees could work and live in pleasant
suburban conditions and enjoy a range of advanced social benefits. No such grand social plan was carried out
in America, but employer concern with benefits,
profit-sharing, and other new ideas for giving workers
some sense of control over their work lives were commonplace in Quaker manufacturing plants. Early in the
history of the labor movement, Quaker businessmen
recognized that unions were essential as a means of
communication between management and workers.
Many saw collective bargaining at its best as similar to
the search for consensus that goes on at Quaker Meetings for Business. Viewed this way, negotiations become a method for bringing about an enlightened
resolution or synthesis of different points of view. One
result is that, by and large, workers at Quaker businesses
have been able to reach fair contract terms without re-
sorting to strikes.

In 1951, a leading member of the Rowntree family
of British Quaker industrialists addressed the subject of
employer-employee relations when he spoke to a group

of American Quaker businessmen. He concluded with a very Quakerly prescription for good labor-management relations that combines high idealism and hard-nosed practicality:

> It is important that industry should be efficient and waste should be reduced to a minimum. The greatest source of waste arises though lack of cordial cooperation between employers and employed. Our aim should be to induce all to work as hard and as intelligently as if they were working for themselves. . . . Remember, there is no such thing as "Labor." The working force is made up of a number of individuals each having a personality different from the rest. They are sensitive as we are to encouragement and discouragement, as easily aroused to anger and suspicion, to loyalty and to effort. One may deal with things without love; but you cannot deal with men without it, just as one cannot deal with bees without being careful. If you deal carelessly with bees, you will injure them, and will yourself be injured. And so with men.

Do these ideas seem simplistic? Naive? Unworkable? Not to the employer who struggles with the high cost of employee turnover. The fact is, many Quaker businesses have demonstrated that profit and social responsibility are not only compatible, but interdependent. Big business enterprises today have become increasingly bottom-line oriented. Rather than being accountable to their customers, they are accountable only to their stockholders. They demonstrate their success not by the public regard they've engendered but by pointing to the figures at the bottom of the profit/loss balance sheet. The Quaker business model seeks cooperation, while recognizing the need to compete. Instead of seeing their workers and customers as adversaries, they view them as partners. Quaker businesspeople understand that they are accountable to the individuals they employ, the customers they serve, the community they share, and their own conscience. Not surprisingly, this adds up to both good citizenship and good business.

The Philadelphia Quartz Company, which makes sodium silicate, magnesium sulfate (Epsom salts), and other chemicals, was established in 1833 by our relatives, the Elkintons and Evanses, some of whom are still active in the company. As far back as anyone remembers, it has been a model Quaker business. In the 1920s, in an effort to emphasize equality, the directors decided that all employees—from the lowest level to the president—were to be referred to by their initials. And all employees, including the president (known to his employees as T.W.E.), began receiving the same annual bonuses. The company's board of directors established a fund to benefit widows or widowers of employees, and their Labor Reserve Fund provided pensions when people retired, years before Social Security came along. The company also established a profit-sharing plan, before these became fairly common, to encourage everyone to become invested in the company's bottom line. Every letter the company sent out bore the salutation "Respected Friend," which became the title of a booklet put out in commemoration of the plant's one hundredth anniversary.

The real bottom line is that everyone wants to buy from people they trust and avoid those they don't. If a manufacturer makes false claims for his products, he does fatal damage to the unspoken covenant with his customers. If an employer reneges on promises to his employee, or if an employee lies to or steals from an employer, suspicion and hostility fill the vacuum created by lost trust. On the other hand, if you treat employees fairly, you will earn their loyalty, and if you deal honestly with your business partners, they will want to continue to do business with you in the future. The same goes for customers. If you offer them goods and services of high quality, they will become repeat buyers. The pursuit of ever larger and faster profits can obscure these basic truths. Business cycles have become so compressed that executives are under tremendous pressure to turn profits every fiscal quarter, at any human cost. It's small wonder that so many businesses suffer from high worker turnover and fickle customers.

The continuously updated Quaker guide to living

and belief, *The Book of Faith and Practice*, makes the case for a cooperative business strategy in few words: "The spirit of brotherhood and service should lead all who are engaged in industry to regard each other not as antagonists struggling to win advantages from each other, but as co-operators, sharing with one another in their common purpose to serve their community."

It doesn't sound like twentieth-century lingo, but through the centuries Quaker businesspeople have followed this advice and found that it works. If we look to the future, we must recognize that merchandising will become increasingly impersonal as we shop even more often in chains rather than in small independent stores. Purchasing via mail-order catalogs and the Internet are likely to become more and more common. But no matter how much the outward appearance of commerce changes, the fundamental human components will always remain the same.

The impersonal, high-speed, complicated nature of modern business appears to leave little opportunity for consideration of the simple, humane values at the root of Quaker business success. But there is evidence to the contrary. I think it's interesting to note that courses in business ethics are taught in the best graduate schools of business, which I see as mainstream acceptance of the principle that good ethics is good business.

As employers, we are still pretty much on our own as we continue to face daily challenges to our conscience, our integrity, our honesty, and our sense of fair play. Will we provide health insurance to employees, even if the law doesn't require it? How "creative" will we be in our accounting? Will we carry employees through hard times, or leave them to fend for themselves?

As employees, we will still need to find meaning and take pride in our work. Will we serve customers poorly or well? Will we create goods and services with care or carelessly? Will we make our daily labor the expression of the best that is in us, or the worst?

And as customers, we will always have to take responsibility for the power of our pocketbooks. We like the idea of supporting a small bookstore or local hardware store, but are we willing to forgo the discounts offered by the chains? Will we buy clothing from a line that exploits its workers? What kind of message will we send a manufacturer who has a history of flouting environmental laws?

Every time we punch a time clock, sign a paycheck, or use a credit card, we have an opportunity to let our life speak.

What do we want to say?

CHAPTER NINE

EDUCATION

TWO AND A HALF centuries ago, Plato, who was re-
nowned as a teacher as well as a philosopher,
wrote: "The direction in which education starts a
person will determine his future life." Most of today's
parents would agree with him wholeheartedly. They
believe that what happens to a boy or girl in school
shapes the *kind* of adult he or she will become. They
are passionately involved in their children's school life;
they volunteer their time to sit on committees, coach
soccer or softball, help in the library, escort classes on
field trips. Many feel that education is too important a
matter to be left simply to teachers—and yet they are
unlikely to agree on the definition of a good school or
a valuable education.

What makes a good school? To me it seems clear
that a good school is one that is constantly engaged in
self-examination, in improving itself, in becoming wiser
in its ability to both teach and inspire. It's a school that

is intent on turning out good people who will help make a better world. It's a school where ideas and ideals are in everyday circulation, the coinage of ordinary transactions.

Those who think of good schools solely in terms of their students' scores on standardized tests miss the point. A school can educate in ways in which its curriculum cannot. It's the soul of a school—its intangible persona, its character, its principles, its daily life over time, the impressions it makes, the efforts it inspires, and the moral authority it possesses—that helps mold a child into an educated, assured, humane, and caring adult. It takes a school—not just bricks and books—to educate a child.

I think it's safe to say that all good schools, like good people and good families, are much alike. I used to think you could tell you were at a Quaker school as soon as you entered because of the cheerful, warm, open, and confident atmosphere engendered by students and faculty. But many good schools, public and private, have the same atmosphere. At a good school teachers and students are jointly engaged in a search for truth, in what Quakers call continuing revelation. Students greet the school day with enthusiasm. Teachers and administrators are there to guide, to respond, to teach, and to learn. They hold high expectations for

their students, knowing that students work toward expectations. And as good teachers grapple with improving the intellectual abilities of their pupils, they also work to provide a climate of sensitivity to the human condition, to ensure that our most personal gift, the gift of our minds, is used in a generous spirit for worthy goals. A good school's overriding aim is to help each student respond to the best that is in him or her.

In some ways it's become much more difficult to educate a child than it was in generations past. Students tote along with them to school, just as surely as they carry their backpacks, a media culture that functions as a highly competitive educational system. It is a culture focused on television, film, advertising, and pop music—media that promote lifestyles that often include drugs, promiscuous sex, and misogyny. It is omnivorous in its consumption of idealism and masterful in its substitution of lesser gods. It seduces our children away from the habit of real thought and substitutes self-absorption and materialism.

Educators are engaged in a contest with the seductive effects of this culture every day, in every classroom and school activity. And yet they are heartened by the openness and fertility of young minds. All teachers know that, just as students may be lured away from the habits that contribute to learning, they are also en-

dowed with optimism and idealism, a far greater sensitivity to their environment than my generation ever had, concern for fairness and decency, openness to new ideas, and tolerance toward those who are different from themselves.

A great debate has been raging in recent years about how to improve our schools. I believe all good schools must recognize that the moral growth of students is at least as important as their intellectual growth. That's what some educators mean when they say that the only proper education is a moral education—which is not to be confused with a sectarian education. The goal of Quaker teachers is to imbue students with the desire to let their lives speak when they graduate and enter the adult world. Non-Quaker educators express the same view somewhat differently when they proudly describe a former student as a productive and useful member of society, an exemplary parent, a warm and responsive human being, an altruist. We can't simply focus on turning out academically well-prepared graduates who will be accepted at the colleges of their choice or enter the workforce with excellent prospects for advancement. Formal education is only a jumping-off point for a lifetime of learning and doing, and what concerns good schools and good teachers is how students apply the learning they acquire to living their lives.

Now, in retirement, I look back at my years of trying to shepherd young minds through the critical transition from childhood to adulthood as the richest period of my life. And I recognize that, in the process, I learned as much as I taught. Being involved on a daily basis with helping young people mature and having a stake in the values they develop always seemed to me the most significant, useful, and interesting enterprise anyone could be involved in.

I trace my own ideas about education back to my early exposure to people who were in love with books and learning. I grew up in a family of passionate readers. Grandfather Stokes, whose tastes were grounded in the classics, read the Latin poets on train trips. My father, who favored nineteenth- and twentieth-century English and American writers, was for many years president of the Ramblers, a Moorestown literary discussion group that invited writers to visit and talk about their work in members' living rooms. I recall as a little boy sitting at the top of the stairs listening to the laughter that emanated from our dining room when Carl Sandburg came to dinner before speaking at the group's meeting. Dad was a big fan of Sandburg, and it was a great occasion for both my parents, who talked about it for weeks afterward Stephen Vincent Benét and Edwin Arlington Robinson were other guests of the Ramblers who came to dinner at our place, and there was no question in my mind—even though I had not yet read their books—that these authors were true heroes.

Dad continually suggested books he wanted us to read, and although as a teenager I used to rebel and insist on picking my own books, his love of words and literature was highly contagious. *Pickwick Papers* was his favorite Dickens novel, and a watercolor of Mr. Pickwick, painted by Dad's mother, hung in a position of honor in our living room for as long as I can remember.

Early in life I was inspired, encouraged, and humbled by my teachers. In the third grade Miss Wildman told me, unwisely, that I was the best student in the class, which buoyed me up for years. But in sixth grade, I was quickly brought down. Miss Swan, considered the top teacher in the school, was also the toughest. She came from Farmington, Maine, and had no time for nonsense. One day when my grandfather, who was clerk of the Meeting's school committee, came for a visit to my class, Miss Swan decided to quiz us verbally on geography. I loved geography and was good at it. I was also always very anxious to confirm Grandfather Stokes's high opinion of my intellect, and in an attempt to let me shine, Miss Swan asked me the first question: "What is the capital of Oregon?" Unfortunately, I had no inkling of the answer. I began to perspire, and as she prodded and hinted, trying to get the right answer out of me but leading me into ever more confusion, I felt totally devastated. To this day I can't pass one of those Salem cigarette billboards without groaning. Grandfather never mentioned my disgrace afterward, but the incident destroyed my intellectual hubris and stayed with me as a reminder that being a good student isn't something that just happens to you; it requires a lot of hard work.

It was my seventh-grade Latin teacher, Mr. Wirt, who really introduced me to the world of ideas. As the class laboriously translated Caesar's *Gallic Wars*, he constantly digressed to talk about themes the text suggested: power and right, the good and bad aspects of the expansion of the Roman Empire, leadership, morality, views on slavery, and the treatment of slaves in ancient times. His was the first classroom in which I'd dealt with big questions that didn't have a right or wrong answer. The class freed my mind. I began *thinking* instead of simply memorizing or calculating.

As a graduate student at Columbia, I attended every lecture given by Mark Van Doren, Lionel Trilling, Jacques Barzun, and Joseph Wood Krutch. These great thinkers and teachers had such an enormous influence on me that I planned for several years to emulate them as a college English professor, but I never completed my Ph.D. degree. With an extremely modest income from part-time teaching and a minor administrative job, and with two children and another on the way, I was unable to take time off to study without interruption for the all-important oral examination required for the degree. I'd been offered a good job at Columbia in undergraduate administration, and in a state of uncertainty and disappointment I visited my graduate adviser, Marjorie Hope Nicholson, the English Department head. Professor Nicholson was a huge and formidable woman, famed as a scholar and also known as a woman of sound and sympathetic judgment. She reminded me that the most influential people of the seventeenth century, my area of concentration, were learned scholars who had devoted themselves to the business of the public good. The advice she gave me led me to the field of academic administration. She urged me to take the job as assistant dean, saying, "If you carry with you all that you've learned here, you will make a valued contribution to the world."

Most of us can look back on some seemingly random occurrence that changed the course of our lives. We marvel at the unlikely meeting with the person who became our husband or wife, or the chance move that took us far enough away from the spot where an artillery shell landed. We may have shifted gears in our life because of something a teacher, friend, or relative said that changed our way of thinking about ourselves. Some people call it fate. Quakers think of it as "way opening." My way opened one day in 1964. I had become an experienced educational administrator at Columbia. Eliza and I had fashioned a happy life for our family in New York. All three of our children—Susie, Katie, and Geoffrey—had been born in Manhattan and were attending excellent schools. But one day, on a train from New York to Philadelphia, I bumped into my cousin Henry Scattergood. Henry, who was fifteen years older than I, had been for some years headmaster of Germantown Friends School, long considered one of the best Quaker schools in the country.

"Did thee know," Henry asked, "that Sidwell Friends is looking for a head? They want a Quaker. Sidwell's a good place. It's where I did my first teaching. Thee'd be good for it. Why doesn't thee try for it?"

In the fall of 1965 I became headmaster of Sidwell Friends School in Washington, D.C., a job that for thirteen years would engage every aspect of who I was. I was bursting with ideas on how it should be done, and the thought of working in close, daily contact with students and teachers seemed to me to be the perfect ticket. In the 1940s I had written a letter to Chester

Reagan, my headmaster at Moorestown Friends School, from an army base in the South. In it I told him that I thought the school hadn't done a very good job of stretching my mind, that it had allowed me to spend too much time on the soccer field. What I didn't tell him was that I had decided that some day, by hook or crook, I'd be a schoolmaster. When, after so many years and changes of direction, I arrived at Sidwell, I was filled with a sense of mission and the thrill of a dream fulfilled.

I was also conscious of the fact that I had a distinguished tradition of Quaker education to uphold, a tradition stretching back to the expansive vision of George Fox, who encouraged the building of Quaker schools as early as 1668, "to instruct young lads and maidens in whatsoever things are civil and useful in creation." Friends believed that women must be as literate as men, that both needed a strong basic education as background for a life of service. Although they established the first coed schools, those early Quakers were not educational theorists. It simply seemed to them that mingling the sexes in the classroom was natural and created the best environment for learning and for later adult participation in communal and family life.

At the end of the seventeenth century there were three coeducational Quaker schools in the colonies, all of which still flourish. Fox proposed that each Meeting start its own school, and by 1750 there were nearly as many of these Quaker primary and secondary schools in the colonies as there are now in the entire country. Because Friends believed in the equality of all people, they also established schools for those who had none—free Negroes, emancipated slaves, and Indians. Colleges and universities were next on the agenda, and in the nineteenth century Haverford, Earlham, and Swarthmore were founded as Quaker colleges, soon to be followed by seven others. Although not under Quaker governance, three other distinguished institutions of higher learning—Cornell, Johns Hopkins, and Bryn Mawr—were started by individual Quakers. The prevailing mission of all Quaker schools was to educate students for society as it ought to be and not for society as it is.

This lofty ideal led me into some pretty deep waters in the turbulent 1960s. Thoughtful people have always agreed that society was in need of improvement, and Quakers have historically mounted formal dissents against social injustice. But during my first decade at Sidwell the right to dissent against perceived wrongs took on new dimensions. In the ferment of the 1960s, students, and faculty as well, heatedly challenged old truths, all authority, and a comprehensive range of social and academic issues from the Vietnam War to study halls.

The center held, but everyone argued the details. An early dispute during my tenure centered on dress code. Boys had always been required to wear jackets and ties; girls wore skirts or dresses. Hair was expected to be tidy and, for boys, of conventional length. But suddenly dress code was condemned as an intrusion on freedom of conscience as well as hypocritical for a Friends school, which was theoretically a bastion of individualism. I confess I was a holdout for the status quo and changed my mind only when it was clear that the dispute was interfering with the more critical aspects of running a school. It seemed to me at the time that the discipline involved in dressing neatly encouraged orderliness of thought and a more serious approach to studies. Most of the students and faculty, and many of the parents, felt differently.

Today, dress codes are a relic of the past, but I still believe that setting some guidelines for student attire is appropriate. While most teenagers perceive clothes and hairstyle as critical forms of self-expression, Quakers have traditionally emphasized expressing the inner self through deeds, not dress. Investing too much of our identity in outward appearance is always a temptation, and the high-decibel fashion statements made by students today can easily overwhelm the quiet voice within.

Obligatory Quaker Meeting, the once-a-week vital centerpiece of all Quaker schools, was suddenly seen by some pupils as an affront to individual liberty. Students demanded that some required courses be dropped and replaced by seminars on the Vietnam War. We did hold some seminars, but we didn't drop any classes. Quaker Meeting continued, and I noted that the more rebellious students were often the ones who gave voice to the most helpful, insightful comments. Many students from this era have told me in recent years that Quaker Meeting—where faculty and students sit down together in silence for about forty minutes to meditate, pray, stir restlessly, share a message from deep within or a more immediate observation—was the most valuable experience of attending a Friends school. I like to think that they still find time for periods of silent contemplation in their busy lives.

One of the things I found out early on was that sometimes a person in authority simply has to make the tough calls and say no in response to a request. This might seem obvious to most people, hardly worth mentioning, but Quakers rarely say no to each other. Their view is that just about any request falls within the reach of compromise and accommodation. When I took up my job as headmaster, I was besieged with requests for special dispensation. Teachers approached me with unorthodox plans for the use of sabbatical time. Students broke the rules and then came before me asking that the usual disciplinary measures be modified or waived. When I found myself in the decision-making position, I recognized that the good of the school community was more important than the wishes of any one person; that despite my concern for individual needs and individual growth—and despite my habit of sifting out the positive and hopeful aspects in every circumstance— often the response that was most consistent with my Quakerly ear for the truth was no.

The 1960s were a stressful time to become a headmaster, but guiding the school through that era was also very gratifying. At no time before or since have idealism and optimism held so much sway with students and teachers. And I can only look with pride at the fine adults, including my own three children, who came of age at our school in those years.

Today, Quakers make up a small minority of the students at all Friends schools, and competition to gain admission is extraordinarily high. What makes Quaker education so valued? And what can Quaker schools teach to those administering public schools?

I think it's significant that a Friends school is always

consciously striving to become a better school community—a process everyone in the school is aware of and involved in. This is an exciting and contagious environment for students, teachers, and parents. One key component is maintaining or increasing diversity—racial, religious, and economic—in the student body and faculty. Without input from people of differing life experiences and cultures, a school quickly becomes insular and intellectually stagnant.

In my opinion, an intellectually stimulating atmosphere also requires the presence of both sexes in the classroom. You can't have an open and informed exchange of ideas if you're lacking representatives of half the population. Some people today advocate a return to single-sex schools where students have fewer distractions and where boys and girls don't have to compete for equal attention. I subscribe to the Quakers' view that school is a preparation for life in the real world. Now that the workplace has grown increasingly coed, it's even more important that schools reflect that reality and prepare young people to deal with a society where women and men must compete and cooperate.

I also feel that Quaker Meeting is a great source of strength and solace for a student body. I am not suggesting that Quaker Meeting be adopted in our public schools, but I do believe that nonsectarian moments of silence help students center themselves amidst the hubbub of the school day. Meeting, or simply periods of silence and centering, can be viewed as the beginning of all learning, because it is in shared silence that we can try to open our minds and listen to our best inner selves. I feel that at school Meetings students get a weekly education of the heart, a practical experience in learning to find the best that is in them. At Meeting students rediscover each week how close and alike they are, and this is a particularly rich reward in schools with a diverse student body. Thirty years ago, when the news of the death of Martin Luther King, Jr., went through our school like a bolt of lightning, all the students spontaneously gathered quietly on the floor of the gym and in the silence—interrupted by brief, poignant words—shared their grief and bewilderment. Over the years since, joining for an impromptu Meeting has continued to offer comfort at times of sorrow or crisis.

Meeting is also a time for introspection and community thinking, a time when a student can work on forming fair and good goals and plans for uses of time. This need not be thought of as a religious exercise but only as a time for standing apart from the outside world to search for one's true self. This is a valuable daily exercise for all of us, but particularly for adolescents, whose sense of identity shifts constantly with the ebb and flow of daily events.

Another characteristic of Quaker schools is that they have involved students in community service at all grade levels, a practice that is now integrated in the curriculum of many other private and public schools. Self-absorption is a hallmark of adolescence, and words about the importance of service—whether they come from the president of the United States or the principal of the high school—mean little if students don't get hands-on experience in helping others and learning from lives and circumstances different from their own. Community service can be, for many boys and girls, the cornerstone of a moral education.

My grandson Christopher, who is twelve, helps out preparing and serving food with his mother, Katie, at a Washington, D.C., shelter called Martha's Table. "When you finish, you feel you've done so much that helps people that you want to keep doing it," he says. "You don't want to leave." I hope Christopher's interest in volunteer work continues, and I believe it will.

Friends schools have other ideas to offer the public schools. Private schools in general can serve as testing grounds for new ideas that might be incorporated later in the public school system. Experimental education is the name of the game in Quaker schools, and they are constantly cooking up new ways of doing things. Because they tend to be smaller and are independently funded, private schools in general are more flexible and can try out innovative programs without extensive bureaucratic involvement. And since private schools must be run economically and make frequent financial reports to their hands-on boards of trustees, they can also offer public schools ideas on how to use funds effectively.

As to curriculum, I believe that the liberal arts remain the heart of an intellectual education. They are "liberating" because studying them frees the mind to think creatively. To read, study, and discuss the best that has been written and thought is to bask in the light of the great minds that have preceded us. "The powers of the person are what education wishes to perfect," Van Doren wrote in his *Liberal Education*, a book that continues to be my educational bible. Friends schools, which are unabashedly in the business of making better people, are built on a belief in the perfectibility of our powers to think clearly and act decisively on our individual convictions.

Fulfilling this ideal requires that we keep the classroom alive with ideas. It also means recruiting great teachers and letting them teach. Teaching is a career that attracts dedicated people of keen intellectual bent who really care about helping kids. While I'm all for paying teachers as much as possible, their real rewards have never been financial. For people who love to teach, the payoff is being granted the autonomy to make your classroom your own private crucible for learning and thinking. Many public school teachers are frustrated by rigid curriculum requirements that totally deprive them of this independence. At Sidwell, teachers are given virtually free rein to express their personal passions, to determine, within their course subject, what to teach and what approach to take, to use their creative energy in the ways they think best.

During my tenure at Sidwell, there was a twelfth-grade teacher who loved Shakespeare's history plays and was passionate about sharing them with her students. She was well aware of the resistance of many students to reading these difficult plays, so she took a novel approach. In her class there were no tests. No term papers. For six months, her students simply read Shakespeare's history plays aloud in class, from *King John* through *Henry VIII*. Several students told me it was the best literature class they'd ever taken, that Shakespeare had never come alive for them before they had the opportunity to "perform" him every day during third period.

Teaching continues to be one of the hardest and most important jobs in the world. There is no formula for imparting love of learning. Despite new methodologies, there must always be reliance on the old virtues of skill, care, love, patience, and time. Young people face an endless series of difficult choices, and the goal of educators is to help give students the confidence and the self-knowledge to make the right decisions as often as possible. In a world of tough choices, nothing less is worth the trouble.

Becoming educated is the only process that engages every human being every day of his or her life. School, as adults come to realize, is only the beginning of learning. What many parents overlook is that education is an all-day and every-day event that begins and ends at home. Longfellow wrote, "A single conversation across the table with a wise man is better than ten years' mere study of books." As often as not that "conversation across a table" takes place during a family's breakfast or dinner, and that "wise man" is usually a father or a mother. Parents are every child's first teachers, and any school, no matter how good, can only build on those first, most formative lessons.

CHAPTER TEN

FAMILY

EARLY ONE OCTOBER AFTERNOON, a few miles north of California's Golden Gate, an intent young couple led a small group of family and friends through a forest of huge redwoods called Muir Woods. They stopped walking when they came upon a place that seemed right, a small grove circled by enormous trees. Branches soared toward the sky, arching and interlacing like the vaulting on a cathedral ceiling, and sun splintered the foliage, lighting up the forest's dark floor. The entire gathering stood there, joined in silence. The Meeting for Worship had begun.

When Eliza felt that the moment had come, she looked up at me and we took each other's hands. Feeling a bit nervous, we recited after each other the single sentence that has been used in Quaker marriages for three hundred years. "In the presence of God and these our friends, I Robert (Eliza) take thee Eliza (Robert) to be my wife (husband), promising with divine assis-

warding, is that over time all of us find ourselves play-ing a variety of roles. We begin by being a son or daughter, but right from birth we are likely to also be a grandchild, a niece or nephew, a cousin, a brother or sister. Later we become spouses, parents, aunts, uncles, grandparents. It's a bit like engaging in an ongoing team sport; each person is required to play his or her desig-nated position, but the positions are constantly shifting. The team must remain united at all times, even when one person is not performing well, is sick or disabled, or is suffering from a loss of spirit. But in one important respect, the sports analogy breaks down. In a family you can't keep score. When family members become in-volved in scorekeeping—who did more of the chores, who banged up the car, who said something harsh years ago that continues to rankle—the team is in trouble.

The gravest problems arise when people feel enti-tled to abandon the team, when they decide it's okay to disconnect from a husband or wife, from parents, from a brother or sister, from elderly and sick grand-parents. That's when the family that may once have been a highly functional unit becomes, in my mind, truly dysfunctional. A strong commitment to maintain-ing bonds of attachment in the face of disruptive life events or inevitable interpersonal conflicts—whether

who never went to a movie herself because of her conviction that all films were somehow tawdry—the title suggested a flamboyantly sexy scenario. Perhaps she was thinking about *The Scarlet Letter*. In any case, the movie was a colorful costume drama, starring Leslie Howard and Merle Oberon, about an Englishman who helped people in danger during the French Revolution. But because of her certainty that I would somehow be corrupted by seeing it, Grandmother gave me the enormous sum of five dollars in exchange for a promise that I would stay away from the movie.

There was, in our music-loving family, only a remnant of the traditional Quaker attitude that held that the arts in general were frivolous, a distraction from the search for truth. This dismissive view of theater, painting, music, novels, and poetry was particularly severe in the late nineteenth century when my father's father was read out of his Meeting for refusing to give up his beloved piano! One result of this prejudice was that Quaker schools, regardless of the degree of excellence they achieved, generally gave short shrift to the arts until recent decades, a situation I worked hard to change in my own school. And, except for Quaker poet John Greenleaf Whittier and the eighteenth-century artists Edward Hicks and Benjamin West, most Friends are hard pressed to come up with the name of

ACKNOWLEDGMENTS

I'm indebted to several people who have helped me transform my ideas into a manuscript, and a manuscript into a book.

The impetus for writing this book came from Joshua Horwitz, a gifted writer and nurturer of other writers. Josh was a student at Sidwell Friends School when I was headmaster, and years later we met in an Old Testament study group. He encouraged me to revive a book I'd been working on about Quaker thought—a project that had gone adrift and was badly in need of a course correction. Josh's skillful, empathetic guidance throughout the crafting of this book has been indispensable.

Any literary distinction this book may possess is due in large measure to Elinor Horwitz. Without her enormous generosity and kindness in sharing her time and superb talents, this book would never have been completed. My thanks to her are beyond measure.

Jamie Stiehm offered many valuable insights and much needed encouragement at the outset of this project, for which I am deeply grateful.

Gail Ross, my agent, contributed both her integrity and her editorial acuity to this project. She's a delight to work with, and a loyal advocate.

I count myself immensely lucky to have Joann Davis as my editor. She has a passion for good books that can do good. With a quick and certain understanding of Quakerism, she saw the book inside my nascent manuscript and skillfully coaxed it into being.

Finally, I'd like to acknowledge the influence on my thinking of one of my great teachers, Mark Van Doren. His mind was serious, his heart was merry, and the whole world was his subject.